P9-CSF-787

ALSO BY HARVEY COX:

Feast of Fools: A Theological Essay on Festivity and Fantasy
God's Revolutions and Man's Responsibility
On Not Leaving It to the Snake
The Secular City
The Seduction of the Spirit: The Use and Misuse of People's Religion
(EDITOR) *Situation Ethics Debate*
(EDITOR) *The Church Amid Revolution*

Turning East

THE PROMISE AND PERIL OF THE NEW ORIENTALISM

Harvey Cox

SIMON AND SCHUSTER
NEW YORK

This book is dedicated to my students at
The Seminario Bautista de Mexico
The Naropa Institute
Harvard Divinity School

Published by Simon and Schuster
A Division of Gulf & Western Corporation
Simon & Schuster Building
Rockefeller Center
1230 Avenue of the Americas
New York, New York 10020
Designed by Edith Fowler
Manufactured in the United States of America
1 2 3 4 5 6 7 8 9 10

Library of Congress Cataloging in Publication Data

Cox, Harvey Gallaher.
Turning east.

Bibliography: p.
Includes index.
1. Cults—United States. 2. United States—Religion. 3. Christianity and other religions. 4. Cox, Harvey Gallaher. 5. Spiritual life—Baptist authors. I. Title.
BL2530.U6C69 200′.973 77-8600
ISBN 0-671-22851-X

Contents

1 Never the Twain

The idea for this book began on the day Harry, Denise and Michael knocked on my front door. It was a quiet Sunday afternoon, and when I opened the door, two young men and a young woman asked if they could come in and talk to me about Krishna. Both the men had shaved their heads, except for a small ponytail at the back. They wore bright saffron robes, simple bead necklaces and sandals. One wore a loose-fitting white shirt-blouse lined with intricate brown-and-blue patterning. Both carried tubular drums encased in woven baskets and ribbons and slung around their necks with broad sashes. The men had two white lines painted on their faces, beginning at the bridge on the nose and running up into their scalps. They told me later this was the sign of *tilaka*, a symbol of the dedication of their bodies to Krishna. All in all they might have looked downright menacing if they had not been smiling. The woman had blue eyes and wore a pale sari, a light shawl and sandals. Her hair was long. She carried finger cymbals and a shoulder pouch stuffed with books and pamphlets. Only later on did I learn that their names were Harry, Denise and Michael. They introduced themselves as Bhārgava dāsa, Krishna Kumari, and Caityaguru dāsa. They were all members of the International Society for Krishna Consciousness, better known as the Hare Krishna movement, and I asked them to come in.

"East is East and West is West," Rudyard Kipling once declared in an often quoted line, "and never the twain shall meet." But as I sat that day and listened to Harry (Bhārgava dāsa), Denise (Krishna Kumari), and Michael (Caityaguru dāsa), I wondered. Harry, it turned out, had been brought up in a liberal Protestant family in Orange, New Jersey. His family, he said, attended church only episodically. They had, however, transmitted to him a "certain feeling for morality" but no very distinct idea of God. Denise had been born into a Jewish family in Brooklyn, had gone to Hebrew school and had recently returned home to attend a younger brother's bar mitzvah. Michael came from a Boston Irish Catholic family, had attended parochial schools for years and had once briefly considered becoming a priest. We talked for an hour, and as we did, my two younger children crept in, stared and then listened attentively as Bhārgava dāsa, Krishna Kumari and Caityaguru dāsa each told about the path that had brought them from the spiritual traditions of their families into the Hare Krishna Movement. As they spoke, Krishna Kumari took some *prasada*—cookies which have first been offered to Krishna—and handed them to the children, who munched them appreciatively. Later, as they arose to leave, the guests offered to give me (though a contribution would of course not be refused) a lushly illustrated English version of the Bhagavad Gita, the Song of God, one of the best known Hindu scriptures, as translated by the founder of their movement, A. C. Bhaktivedanta Swami Prabupada. I accepted, and as the visitors wended their way further down the street, drumming, clinking the cymbals and chanting "Hare Krishna," I noticed my children eagerly poring through the pages of the Bhagavad Gita and staring at the pictures of sky-blue Krishna and the dark-eyed cow-maidens of Vrindaban.

The unexpected Sunday visit puzzled me. Who were these strange visitors from so near and yet so far away? Were they purblind fanatics, confused adolescents, the brainwashed victims of some hypnotic cult leader? As we talked, they had not seemed like any of these. What were they, then? Was this the meeting of East and West that Kipling thought would not take place until both eventually stood at "God's great judgment seat"?

As a child I had scarcely heard of religions other than Christianity and Judaism. I had certainly never met any adherents of them. My initial encounter with the Bhagavad Gita came in a college sophomore comparative religion course. Now all that seemed to be changing. The Orient, or at least some of its Western representatives, was now literally knocking on my door, and the Gita lay open on the living-room floor. East and West were beginning to intersect in ways that neither Rudyard Kipling nor I had anticipated.

The Hare Krishna devotees themselves represented only a small group, but they are a part of something larger and much more significant—a wave of interest among Americans in Oriental spirituality whose scope and intensity is unprecedented in the history of American religion. True, a degree of fascination with the East has existed in America since at least the early nineteenth century. Ralph Waldo Emerson and Walt Whitman both read the Gita. Emerson published a Hindu-inspired poem called "Brahma," and his transcendentalist philosophy includes elements that sound distinctively Hindu, such as the idea of the "Oversoul." This early nineteenth-century wave of Indian thought not only influenced transcendentalists; it also created movements like Theosophy and the Unity School of Christianity. In the latter part of the century, a second wave of influence occurred. The famous Swami Vivekananda arrived in 1893 from India and founded the Vedanta Society, which still exists today. The influence of Oriental spirituality in the West is hardly something new.

But there is something new about the present situation. In previous decades, interest in Oriental philosophy was confined mostly to intellectuals and was centered largely on ideas, not on devotional practices. There is no evidence that Emerson ever sat in a full lotus. Today, on the other hand, not only are large numbers of people who are in no sense "intellectuals" involved, but they appear more interested in actual religious practices than in doctrinal ideas. The recent wave of interest in Oriental forms of spirituality seems both broader and deeper than the ones that preceded it.

As I began to look into this remarkable new development in American religious history, and to ask myself what it meant, I quickly noticed something else: the town I live in provides an extraordinarily fertile field for pursuing an inquiry into neo-Oriental religious movements. Cambridge, Massachusetts, was blessed by its English colonial founders with a name derived from their old university, and designed to suggest civility and higher learning. It is the home of Harvard, the oldest university in America. But in recent years Cambridge has also become something its Calvinistic founders could hardly have foreseen. It is one of the four or five most thriving American centers of the neo-Oriental religious surge. This should not be surprising, since Cambridge is full of just the kind of people to whom these movements appeal—mainly young, usually white, and almost always of middle-class background. An acquaintance of mine, recently returned from Benares, the Holy City of India, where millions come to bathe in the sacred waters of the Ganges, took a look around Cambridge last year and promptly rechristened it, "Benares-on-the-Charles."

The analogy is an apt one. Within twenty blocks of the intersection of Massachusetts Avenue and Boylston Street, forty or fifty different neo-Oriental religious movements thrive. A few blocks west stands the Zen center, furnished with black silk cushions, bells, an appropriately wizened and wise-looking resident master, and a visiting Zen swordplay instructor. In the other direction, in the basement of a hospitable Episcopal church, the Sufi dancers meet twice a week to twist and turn like the legendary whirling dervishes in a ritual circle dance, chanting verses from the Koran, the Muslim holy book, in atonal Arabic. A few blocks to the northeast is the Ananda Marga center, located in a large gray frame house on a maple-lined residential street, and specializing in a combination of meditation and community action. If one is ready for a deep plunge into imported odors and colors, one seeks out a few blocks to the south the headquarters of my Sunday visitors, the Hare Krishnas, officially known as the International Society for Krishna Consciousness. There the devotees hold a weekly feast of savory Indian food and a somewhat less piquant introductory lecture on the mysteries of the Krishna devotion. The clean-shaven followers of the young guru Maharaj Ji's Divine Light Mission have a meeting place ten blocks southeast, near Central Square. Recently a group of self-styled Sikhs, immaculately clad in white robes, turbans and wrist daggers, have opened a vegetarian restaurant near the shore of the Charles, called the Golden Temple of Conscious Cookery. One should not overlook the nearby International Student Meditation Center, founded several years ago by the Maharishi Mahesh Yoga, the best known of the swamis of the late sixties, where one can go to be initiated into the mysteries of TM. More recently, the followers of Sri Chinmoy, the former postal clerk guru who lives in Queens, have begun to be more in evidence. There is also Dharma House, eleven blocks north, founded recently by Chogyam Trungpa Rinpoche, the Tibetan Buddhist lama. And there are dozens of smaller, less stable groups, countless Yoga centers, Tai Chi exhibits and sitar concerts. When one adds them all together, the picture of Cambridge as an intellectually prim university town fades as the image of a hive of neo-Oriental religious fervor begins to take its place.

What has provoked this Oriental religious revival? Who are the people who find themselves caught up in it? Why have they left either some more conventional Christian or Jewish form of religious life—or no religious life at all—to become seekers or adherents in these new spiritual movements? What does it all mean for American culture and for Christianity?

When these questions began to puzzle me after the visit of the Krishna disciples, I decided to devote some of my own energy and to enlist my students into looking for the answers. Eventually, I thought, I might even write a book on the subject. Some of the students were already involved in one or another neo-Oriental practice and were eager to learn more. Most were just curious about what the movements meant to their adherents, why they had joined, what they were looking for. Consequently they were ready to visit, observe, participate in meetings and rituals, talk with devotees, and then pool their findings with the experiences of fellow students.

There was still a problem, however. I recognized that even though my home town provided a marvelous field of inquiry into the new Orientalism, and my students were eager to help, one very formidable obstacle remained. The obstacle was me. I could not afford to overlook the fact that, ever since my late teens, I have had a standing suspicion of excessively "inward" and socially passive religions. Especially since my college years, when I left a pietistic student religious organization because of its members' sanctimonious Toryism, I have steered clear of any religion that seemed to give people an excuse for withdrawing from the pain and confusion of the world. I had been intellectually converted from my own fundamentalism in my junior year in college by reading Reinhold Niebuhr's *Moral Man and Immoral Society* with its withering exposure of pietistic individualism. In my years of graduate study, I developed an admiration for Paul Tillich, who always considered himself a "religious socialist," and for Walter Rauschenbusch, the prophet of the American social gospel. Later I came to admire the Reverend Martin Luther King, Jr., and still later I became acquainted with the various schools of "liberation theology," including those emanating from the Catholic left of Latin America. This personal history made me very suspicious, at least initially, of the neo-Oriental wave, and I knew that, no matter how hard I tried to maintain scholarly objectivity, my inner distrust for all "opiates of the people," East or West, might continue to influence me, if mainly on the unconscious level. Even in my own judgment I did not seem to be the right person to carry out a fair and impartial study of something which many people saw as a massive retreat from the social activism of the previous decade.

After giving the problem of my own possible bias a lot of thought, I decided to do the study anyway. I was just too curious about the new movements to ignore them, and I desperately wanted to answer the questions they raised in my mind. Also, although my prejudice against some of the movements was undeniable, I was at least fully aware of it and could take it into consideration in any judgments I would make. Furthermore, as one colleague assured me when I asked for advice on this issue, anybody who is interested enough in anything to spend time learning about it inevitably has *some* feelings about it. Consequently, after I spent some preliminary weeks along with my students scouting out the turf, we screwed up our collective courage and plunged into our "field," the Benares-on-the-Charles.

During the first several weeks of the study we all had a marvelous time. Together and separately we attended dozens of meditation sessions, feasts, satsangs, introductory lectures, inquirers' meetings, worship services and study circles. We asked questions, read mounds of tracts and pamphlets, watched, listened and filled up countless tape cartridges. The students enjoyed the enterprise, and so did I. For once we were getting some things straight from the source instead of from the textbooks. And the groups we visited were invariably hospitable and open to our questions. What I would later refer to as Phase One, of three distinct phases of the study, was well under way.

As our work continued, we began to collate the answers people gave to our questions about why they had begun to participate in such movements. Many of the people we spoke with expressed a need for friendship or community, some antidote to loneliness. They seemed to have found in their fellow practitioners a degree of companionship they had not found elsewhere. Others told us they had wanted to learn a discipline or practice—chanting, meditating, bodily exercise—which they claimed had brought them into immediate touch with God or spiritual reality, or themselves, or something from which they had previously felt separated. Still others told us they had turned East because of their dissatisfaction with one or another aspect of Western religion, or because they simply needed a clear spiritual authority to make some sense out of their lives.

These answers were all interesting enough, but by the end of the semester I felt that something was lacking. I could understand the words people were saying to us, but somehow the key dimension seemed missing. Little by little, as the notebooks piled up, I began to wonder what it would feel like to be on the *inside* of one of the movements. Is such a feeling ever available to outsiders? No one can hope to know another person's God as she does, nor experience his faith as he does. As a Christian and a professional theologian, I realized I was neither a genuine Oriental pilgrim nor an authentic seeker. I was intrigued, curious, fascinated; but I was not a devotee. Still, I began to see that I would have to pursue some kind of "inside" knowing and feeling if I were going to understand the disciples I was studying. So I tried another method.

In this, Phase Two of my work, I tried to become as much of a participant as I could. I was still an investigator, but I no longer simply hovered on the edge of things. I did not merely observe the Sufi dancers, I whirled too. I did not just read about Zen, or visit centers; I "sat." I chanted with the Hare Krishnas. I stood on my head, stretched my torso and breathed deeply with the Yoga practitioners, and spent hours softly intoning a mantra to myself in a favorite form of Hindu devotional practice. I became a participant, not because I thought there was actually something in it for me, but because I wanted to nourish my capacity for empathy. I wanted to find out what I could about the lure of the East on the visceral level. This participant-observer phase of my inquiry, I should add, took me far away from Benares-on-the-Charles. It led me to spiritual centers in California, Texas and Vermont, and into long conversations with Zen abbots, Sufi drummers and Divine Light devotees. Eventually this second phase of my search brought me to Boulder, Colorado, where my investigation took a completely unexpected turn: Phase Two ended and Phase Three began.

I find it hard to characterize Phase Three. In the previous stages of participant-observation research, I had always continued to be more an observer than a participant. True, I had long since gone beyond simply reading descriptions and asking questions, but even in the dancing, the chanting and the breathing I retained a certain inner distance. It was all designed to make me a better observer and commentator. I was still asking what it all meant for other people, for the church, or for Western society. I was not asking what it meant for me, and I could not imagine myself as an East Turner.

Then something I had not anticipated happened. I discovered that when someone is studying beehives up close, regardless of how much inner distance is retained there is still a distinct possibility that the investigator can be stung. While trying to find out what it would feel like to be an East Turner, I found myself—contrary to all my expectations and prejudices—"turning East." While wondering what kind of personal void an Orientally derived spiritual discipline might fill in someone's life, I discovered something that filled a previously unnoticed void in my own. Almost without noticing what was happening, I slipped across the border between "them" and "us." Consequently, a book which had started out as sympathetic description became, at least in part, critical autobiography.

I did not become a convert. I have not shaved my head, adopted an exclusively brown-rice diet or taken up public chanting and drumming. In the course of my investigation, however, I became aware that many of the hopes and hungers that motivate people to turn toward the East were not just observable in others: they were also present in me. I believe, in fact, that nearly everyone in our society feels them in some measure. But I went a little further. I also discovered that at least one of the spiritual disciplines taught by one of the neo-Oriental movements—in my case it was the meditational practice taught by the Tibetan Buddhists in Colorado—met a deep, if previously unrecognized, need in my own life. Although I rejected nearly all the theological trappings the Buddhists have attached to meditation, the "shamatha" practice itself became an integral part of my life.

Now I had to cope with a difficult decision. Since the Turn East had become a personal rather than a merely professional consideration for me, I had to face the same problem I had struggled with earlier, this time from the other side. I considered the idea of discarding the book altogether. Since my study had unexpectedly come to mean so much to me personally, once again I had to ask how I could possibly be "objective." Even worse, would writing a book somehow undercut the subjective importance my quest had taken on? Troubled by both of these questions, I went back and reread all my notes. I was greatly relieved. I discovered as I went through the material again that, although I could now grasp the meaning of things that had eluded me before and could understand the whole Turn East much better, I was *not* more sympathetic. In fact, at certain points I was more suspicious. Contrary to what many social science theories insist, my being more or less "inside" the Turn East did not make me any less capable of sensing its dangers or noticing its foibles. To my great surprise, my own Turn East made me even more critical, and in rereading my earlier notes, I could now see why.

Before the change in my own perspective occurred, I had been going out of my way to see the best side of it all. Knowing my original anti-pietistic bias, I had been giving the benefit of every possible doubt to the Turn East, even to the point of repressing my hunches about impostors and humbug if the evidence was not unambiguously clear. I had been leaning over backward to be fair. After all, who wants to be accused of performing a hatchet job on someone else's religion? I had been a model of academic restraint and objectivity. Consequently, my conclusions had been tepid, commendably moderate, and above all, dull. After my involvement became personal, however, most of the scholarly restraint disappeared. I could give voice to my most troubling suspicions about many, indeed most, aspects of the Turn East, and I could express my anxieties about how badly Oriental teachings are misunderstood and misused in the West.

Furthermore, my other fear—that writing the book would endanger the personal reality of what I had found—also faded. Despite the popular belief that writing or talking about something invariably spoils it, I found that the attempt to describe my experience with the Turn East made it more real and more vivid. Without doubt there are mystical ascents and ecstatic visions that defy mere words, but my experience with the Tibetan practice of meditation had been nothing like that. In fact, it had been nearly the opposite—sane, clarifying, grounding, "ordinary." Furthermore, even though the inner essence of wordless meditation obviously cannot be described in words, one can say a lot about what the experience means for the rest of life. I have never liked the idea of *sacrificium intellectus*—that certain experiences, usually religious ones, require us to immolate our minds. Admittedly, language is an imperfect tool, but however imperfect it is, we must still use it to relate some parts of our lives to other parts and to share our experiences with our fellow human beings. I have found that writing about the spiritual discipline I learned has not eviscerated it, but has integrated it more fully into my life.

Not only did my experience with Buddhist meditation give me a clearer insight into both the perils and the possibilities of the new Orientalism; it also provided me with a central clue to the inner meaning of the whole phenomenon—something I had just not been able to find before. Now, as I look back, I can easily see why the clue had been so elusive. Indeed, how can anyone make sense out of the jumble of movements and the confusion of religious ideas and sentiments which I have lumped together under the phrase "the Turn East"? At first glance the problem of finding a focus seems nearly impossible. There are hundreds of neo-Oriental movements flourishing in America today, ranging in size from ambitious national networks down to tiny handfuls of disciples of this or that teacher. Here a quiet cabal gathers to listen to a tape of Ram Dass. There a study circle pores over the Lotus Sutra. Groups seem to appear and disappear overnight. Gurus come and go. Teachings and practices blend and overlap. Serious masters, parvenus and outright charlatans fly in and out. How can an inquirer sort through the confusion in an orderly way?

I began to study the Turn East as a confused, nearly bewildered, observer. I needed a map, and I tried two or three without hitting on one that satisfied me. Ordinarily I might have chalked up the failure of the first couple of maps to the initial difficulties one always encounters in trying to see patterns in what appears to be a hopelessly scrambled scene. But in this instance, I think, in retrospect, that my initial frustrations were helpful, because they eventually taught me something about the neo-Oriental movements themselves. The fact that they could not be adequately studied with the normal methods of religious research reveals a critical facet of their reality. New wine bursts old wineskins. Something is going on that the standard methods and categories cannot explain.

For example, it first seemed sensible to me to divide the movements into groups corresponding to the original religious traditions to which they claimed to be related. I called this the "great traditions" approach. But after I had sorted out dozens of groups and movements into the three categories of Hindu, Buddhist and Muslim, plus a special category for Sikhs, it was obvious that I did not understand the neo-Oriental phenomenon any better than I had before. The trouble was that what I had learned about Oriental religions in my previous years of reading their sacred texts and investigating their history seemed to have little connection with what was happening in Benares-on-the-Charles. People who claimed to be immersed in Hindu practices often seemed amazingly unfamiliar with the Hindu scriptures. Enthusiastic Zen disciples sometimes seemed to know very little about Buddhist philosophy. I talked with Sufi dancers who, though they could chant phrases from the Koran for hours, while twirling to staccato drums, had no inkling of what the words actually meant. One perspiring young dervish dancer, who told me she had been born Jewish, seemed a little nonplussed when I pointed out to her that the Arabic words she had been chanting all evening meant "There is no God but Allah, and Mohammed is his prophet."

The problem presented by trying to map neo-Oriental movements in relation to the classical traditions is that of radical adaptation. Adaptation takes place whenever a religious tradition travels to a new setting, but it seems to have reached new limits of elasticity in America. The fact is that most of the movements I looked into have altered the Oriental original so profoundly that little can be gained by viewing them in the light of classical ancestry. They are far more "neo-" than "Oriental." Their leaders have stirred in such generous portions of the occult, of Christian images and vocabulary, and of Western organizational patterns, that trying to understand them in relation to an older "mother tradition" can ultimately be quite misleading. By now most of them are Western movements and are best understood as such.

It took a real Asian to show me just how far this Americanizing of Oriental religions can go. The lesson came when a student from India, who is a Sikh, asked me for permission to write a research paper on a group of American young people who have organized the Boston branch of something called the 3 HO (Happy, Holy, Healthy Organization), which was started in America by a Sikh teacher named Yogi Bhajan. Sikhism is an independent Indian religious movement which was founded by Guru Nanak (A.D. 1469–1539), who was a vigorous opponent of ritualism and the caste system. It differs considerably from any form of Hinduism. Sikhs are easily recognizable because of their practice of not cutting their hair and of wearing large turbans and tiny wrist daggers. My turbaned Indian student spent several weeks getting to know these young American "Sikhs" well. He visited their commune, attended their services and talked with them at some length individually. Afterwards he wrote an informative and sympathetic paper on the group. He had learned to like them all very much. But he also concluded that their religious practice and ideas bore only the faintest resemblance to the Sikh teachings he had been reared on his whole life. Although the outward forms appeared similar —these young people also let their hair grow and wore turbans and wrist daggers—the meaning they attached to these practices turned out to be a mixture of astral metaphysics and esoteric lore completely unfamiliar to the young Indian, who wrote with good humor that his fellow Sikhs in India would be very surprised to learn that in the 3 HO movement the long hair is gathered on the forehead and covered by a turban to protect a particularly sensitive area of the brain from malignant cosmic rays. Obviously, studying this group in terms of classical Sikhism would cause more confusion than clarification.

So I junked the "great traditions" map of neo-Oriental religious movements. For a time my thinking seemed to lack any focus, and the task appeared impossible. Then I considered comparing the various movements in terms of *how much* they had adapted themselves to American culture. On one end of such a scale would stand those movements which almost seem to have been invented and distributed to appeal to the Western mind. Surely the Transcendental Meditation movement and the Divine Light Mission of the Maharaj Ji, which has its own Telex system and public-relations firm, would be located near this "high adaptation" border. These groups seem much more Western than Indian.

At the other edge one could place those movements which retain such a dense Oriental ethos that only a very small number of Westerners can find access to them. The Hare Krishna people, who not only wear distinctive costumes and try to learn Sanskrit, but also create a miniature Indian religious subculture, would belong at this nonadaptation end. Most groups range somewhere in the middle.

I soon discovered, however, that this degrees-of-adaptation scheme had its pitfalls, too. The problem is that there are various *kinds* of adaptation. Some movements conscientiously try to relate themselves to specifically Western modes of thought. Others seem to have been redesigned merely to increase their sales appeal. Some of the movements, the Zen Buddhist, for example, appear able to adapt very well in the realm of outside forms while retaining an impressive "inner" authenticity. Most of the movements are a hodgepodge of "authentic" and "adaptive" elements. So much for map number two.

It was not until after my own Turn East that I finally hit on an approach which seemed both faithful to the movements and helpful in interpreting them to other people. I had made my own Turn East for personal reasons. I had also made it with a host of internal reservations and for purposes that were quite different from the ones advanced by the teachers themselves. I was quite sure that mine was a most unusual case. I soon discovered, however, that it was not. Once I got to know them, it turned out that many of the people I met in these movements were there for personal reasons that often had little to do with the official teachings of their leaders. This was an astonishing and humbling discovery, but it did provide me with the clue I needed. I decided to avoid long descriptions of the movements or of the leaders or even of the ideas taught by the neo-Oriental groups. These are covered in other books anyway. I decided instead to focus on the people themselves. I decided to concentrate not on what the movements and their leaders claim to offer but on what the individuals who turn to them actually find. The two are often quite different. This approach finally seemed to make sense of my own experience. I had found something in one of the movements which was both relevant to my own life history and different from anything the literature had prepared me to find. I suspected the same was true for other people as well, and soon found that it was.

This book then is the record of a journey which began as a tour and turned into a pilgrimage. It describes what happened to an investigation that became a discovery. It recounts what took place as I moved from onlooker to actor, from describer to partaker. It concludes with a section on what it all taught me about the meaning of the Turn East for American society and for the American Christian churches in particular. Throughout the book I use the term "neo-Oriental" to indicate that I am not talking in these pages about the great Eastern traditions themselves, about Hinduism or Buddhism as they exist in their Asian settings. That would be another book. I am talking about the American versions of these traditions, which have begun, literally, to knock on our front doors, and about what they mean to the people who find something in them.

I have not seen Harry, Denise or Michael since the day they knocked at my door. I do not know if they still belong to the Hare Krishna group. They may not. In any case, I am grateful to them and I hope that wherever they now are in their pilgrimages, things are going well for them. They helped start me along a path which took a totally unexpected course. The journey I made, while helping me to appreciate more deeply what the East has to teach us today, also made me in some ways more Christian than I had been at the beginning. My guess is that the same thing, or something very similar, will happen to a lot of us before many more years go by.

2 The Sound of One Hand: Confessions of a Zen Drop-Out

My journey to the East began with a five-minute walk. When I moved into Phase Two of my inquiry and decided to explore the Turn East as a participant rather than simply as an observer, the next question was where, in the teeming Benares-on-the-Charles, to start. The easiest course was obviously to begin with the place closest to home. I did not have to go far. Two blocks from my doorstep, near the entrance to the A & P parking lot, stands a hulking gray frame house surrounded by high hedges. It shelters a group of very ordinary-looking young Americans—no shaved heads or saris—who are seriously engaged in the practice of Zen. I had already visited their center a few times in the first phase of the study, and they had always invited me to come back any time and "sit" with them; so one day I rang their doorbell and asked if I could join them in sitting. Phase Two was under way.

There are dozens of Zen centers in America, and they all look innocent enough. But beware of that first visit. The plainness, the lack of exotic decor, the friendliness of the residents could not be better designed to intrigue and frustrate the seeker. "What do you actually do during your sitting sessions?" I asked the young man who showed me in. "We sit," he said, "we just sit." He was right, as I soon learned for myself. One enters and is warmly welcomed by the residents (in this center, all Americans). One is given minimal instructions on how to sit cross-legged on a black silk cushion facing the wall, and then one sits and sits and sits some more, with short breaks only for silent meals. It is often boring and frustrating and—in terms of what our society deems useful—undeniably a total waste of time.

Then why do it? The answer is not what one "learns" from sitting: how it calms, focuses, centers or mellows people. The answer is no "answer" at all. Even to report what happened when I sat hour after hour, looking at a wall, hardly seems to be an answer. What happened is that my back began to hurt and my legs to ache. My mind wandered. I fidgeted. Fugitive thoughts somersaulted through my head, chased by my ineffective efforts to exclude them. Snatches of songs blew playfully into my ear. Things I had to do assumed pained faces in my mind and glanced conspicuously at their watches. I tried harder, and only very slowly, through many sessions of just sitting, did I find out that trying to exclude these cerebral intruders is just as useless and invalid as paying attention to them. Ever so slowly I learned how to let them scamper at will without either censoring them or surrendering to them, without interfering or identifying. Of all the writers about the Zen novice's ordeal, Claudio Naranjo puts it best:

> In trying not to do anything, the first thing that the meditator will probably have to "do" is to stop trying. The issue will take him into paradoxical situations: thinking is a deviation from the assignment of non-doing, but so is any attempt to prevent the arising of thought. The way out, again, is not anything he can "do," but rather it is in the nature of a *realization*, a shift in point of view. It lies in the discovery that from the very beginning he has not done anything, and there is nothing he can do, however much he tries. . . . (Naranjo, 1972, p. 145)

Zen has sometimes been called an "asceticism of the mind," in contrast to the more familiar asceticisms of the bodily appetites. In one way this is true. Zen bears many of the marks of athletic training, and one Zen meditator who had run cross-country at college told me the two seem quite similar to him—that toward the end of a race he often became an observer watching his body stagger toward the finish, knowing somehow that if he fully entered that body and felt what it was feeling, he couldn't take another step. So with the Zen practitioner. He wants to limit the boisterous aspirations of consciousness, to school it in humility, to encourage it to watch its own processes, neither claiming them for its own nor disclaiming them. Yet in another way Zen meditation is not ascetic at all, at least not in the classical sense of a spirited wrestling match, an attempt to subdue and control. Quite the opposite—Zen seeks to allow all thoughts or none, neither embracing nor eschewing them. In "sitting," the hard part lies not, as many suppose, in *controlling* vagrant thoughts, but rather in seeking *not* to control them.

It is ironic that my first direct experience of the Turn East is also the most difficult to describe. Of all the movements I tried to learn about during this quest, the one that annoyed me and appealed to me most was Zen. No discipline came as close to persuading me of its validity; and, paradoxically, no other seemed as remote and unapproachable. The hours I spent in Zen meditation were both the most rewarding and the most frustrating, the most illuminating and the most unbearably boring. The "philosophy" of Zen, if that is what it can be called, seemed at the same time the most sensible and also the hardest to understand. This is why I find it so difficult to write *about* Zen. Even as the words appear on the page, I can hear the laughter of ten thousand masters and teachers echoing around me. The cascades of mirth arise from the Zen practitioner's sublime awareness that although Zen is one of the most fascinating of all the Oriental movements to "come West," no one has ever adequately described it in words.

Zen is a word shredder. It chews concepts to bits and spits out the fragments. But it is equally impossible to describe the "experience" of Zen. Unlike many other practices, Zen is not something one can describe as an "experience." The roshis, or masters, apply a simple, direct treatment to the innocents who come to Zen seeking "experience": they swat them with fans. Zen is not at all congenial to that avarice for experience which has begun to replace the old-style material gluttony in the West. Maybe that is why Zen attracts such an enormous number of curiosity seekers, and also why few novices stick with its rigorous disciplines very long.

One who comes to Zen with the desire to "experience" anything, including satori, or enlightenment, will eventually discover that Zen neither promises nor produces an experience of anything. Through its demanding disciplines one learns that all a person really needs to experience is the experience that one needs to experience nothing. Here then is a practical philosophy that manages to belittle both religious doctrine and religious experience, that provides no stated rituals, no heaven or hell, no God (and no "no-God"), and that offers no obvious ethic, since it sees such categories as "good" and "evil" as imposed and deceptive.

To the Western mind Zen seems to exemplify the mirror opposite of everything Western civilization affirms. It has no interest in results, finds such words as "aim" or "intention" misleading, undermines any sense of achievement or accomplishment and encourages an attitude in which even succeeding at Zen itself would be a kind of failure. "Success" and "failure" belong to the world of illusion. The books of Zen stories and sayings overflow with anecdotes about disciples who, just as they think they have succeeded in this or that Zen discipline, are tweaked on the nose or bashed on the back by the roshi—to remind them again that succeeding in Zen is not the way of Zen.

No wonder that by a curious twist of history this obscure Oriental sect called Zen has become a household word in America. It is the Dr. Jekyll of the West's Mr. Hyde, or, maybe, vice versa. Societies, like individuals, develop some traits at the expense of others. But the repressed elements never simply die. They lurk there in the psyche, seeking some means of expression. Consequently, every people harbors a fretful fascination for its polar opposite, its "shadow self." Zen Buddhism attracts and infuriates the Western spirit, seduces and rebuffs it at the same time. As the yin of the Western yang, its power to fascinate Western minds is infinite.

The word "Zen" itself is Japanese, derived from the Chinese "Ch'an," which refers to a particular form of meditation. Over the years, however, "Zen" has also come to signify the ultimate Void, the All-Mind or No-Mind that Buddhists believe is the basic reality. It also refers to the human awareness of this ultimate. Yet, desipte the word's ancient derivation, the Zen masters insist that Zen is not a form of meditation at all. Father Heinrich Dumoulin, a Jesuit scholar who has written *The History of Zen Buddhism,* calls it a "natural mysticism," but Zen practitioners would probably guffaw just as boisterously at this label as they do at all the others Westerners try to attach to Zen. Let us then simply say that Zen is a tradition of spiritual and psychological disciplines coming to us from China by way of Japan. For fifteen hundred years these disciplines have helped people to reach a form of consciousness which enables them to live serenely without withdrawing themselves from the everyday world of work, conflict and aggravation.

How does it happen? Although many Zen followers would stoutly deny it, and although one important school of Zen, the Soto school, does not use them at all, I believe the Zen sayings, or "Koans," remain the most helpful clue for Westerners to the method and mystery of Zen. A koan is a word, a riddle or a phrase that is generally given to a Zen initiate by the master as the focus for meditation. A koan has no answer or solution in any conventional meaning of those words. The most famous of these koans in the West is "What is the sound of one hand clapping?"—a question which either has an obvious, too obvious, answer or else has none at all. But for this very reason, the koan illustrates both the "Zen method" *and* the difficulty which all minds, not just Western ones, have with Zen. Here is a typical description given by Christmas Humphreys, a recognized Western authority on Zen, of his arduous and rattling encounter with the koan his master gave him.

> The mind wraps itself round the given koan by night and day for weeks and months without end. First, the intellect tries to solve it and fails. Then, it is sucked dry of symbolism, analogy and metaphor. And so through endless methods the mind tries to solve the insoluble. Meanwhile the tension grows; the engine of thought is forced down a narrowing corridor with high walls on either side—only to face a high wall at the end. The pressure grows; the pupil sweats and is sleepless with effort, while the master watches, as a doctor over a woman in travail, helping where he can, controlling where he must. (Humphreys, 1949)

Humphreys is so impressed with the lethal potency of the koan that he strongly warns against its use if there is no master present to preside over the travail. He urges us not simply to "have a go" at Zen without an experienced master at hand. Minds can snap, he reminds the reader, and some of the keenest have been known to fall apart in the struggle with the koan.

It seemed to me that Humphreys was exaggerating. Besides, who can resist the temptation to have at least a little bit of a "go" at a koan, especially after such a dire prediction? So, without any roshi's having given it to me, and without the immediate supervision of a master, I decided one day, after a month of occasionally sitting at the Zen center, to try to meditate for a few weeks on "What is the sound of one hand clapping?" Selecting that particular koan was doubtless a terrible choice, not just because I chose it myself rather than having it given me by a roshi, but also because it is so well known that it has almost become a cliché. Yet, I reasoned, if Zen is what it purports to be, then precisely the most banal and conventional koan was what I needed most. So I plunged in, finding a cushion, selecting a blank wall and meditating every day, sometimes at the Zen center and sometimes at home, on "What is the sound of one hand clapping?"

I could never record the numberless digressions and byways my mind traversed during those harrowing sessions. Nor my efforts first to exclude digressions and then not to exclude them. I was too sly to try to solve the riddle conceptually, and I started out by taking a certain pride in my shrewdness. On further reflection, however, I realized that the answer "This question has no answer" is itself an answer, and a resoundingly sensible one at that. So that response had to be discarded. As the days went on, I then turned to the meanings of "sound" and "one" and "hand" and "clapping." I spent a whole morning in meditation on "one" and nearly two on "hand." I waded through inversions and substitutions. Anagrams came to mind, reversals, varied intonations ("*What* is the sound . . . ?" "What *is* the sound . . . ?"). I rehearsed all the ways the question could be asked: analytically, angrily, desperately, factually, condescendingly. (For a long time I was sure it was condescendingly, even a little nastily: a way for my nonexistent roshi to cut me down to size.) As a recess relief, I played with the tone of the letters, the sibilance of the s's, the popping of the p's, the long way your lips travel to say "what." Then my renditions of the question became more desperate. Should I sing it, sob it, shriek it, chant it?

I began to marvel at the absurdity of the whole enterprise. I glowered inside at Christmas Humphreys, at Zen Buddhism, at the various masters of the koan-using Rinzai school of Zen, at pretentious anti-intellectual absurdities, and at myself for reaching such an impasse. Worst of all now, the koan, instead of being something I tried to meditate on while other thoughts knocked at the windows, became a persistent visitor who would not leave, even when invited, and who hovered around my head when I was in no mood to meditate. The koan became my own little surrogate of Martin Luther's pestiferous demon, leering at me impishly wherever I looked, bulging its eyes and thrusting out its tongue, inviting me to hurl an inkwell at it, as Luther did.

Finally, after several weeks of mounting fury and anxiety, I quit. I knew that I had gone far enough so that the next step would no longer be "having a go" at Zen, but "being had" by Zen. I remembered the Zen teaching that at some point the student *becomes* his or her koan, and I decided that at this point strategic retreat was the better part of spiritual valor. No doubt Humphreys is right. To pursue Zen any further I would need a master.

Let us set aside as entirely un-Zen any consideration of whether I "succeeded" or "failed" in my tiny venture into Zen koan meditation. Let us also set aside what Mr. Humphreys or any of the other tens of thousands of Westerns students of Zen would say about my exercise—namely, that it had nothing to do with Zen at all. For if what they say most of the time about Zen has any validity, then there is nothing in the world that has nothing to do with Zen. Also, although my description of my first tryst with a koan may sound flip and irreverent (both of which, however, are Zen virtues), it did give me a small sense of the enormous power the Zen masters are pointing to.

As a failed student of Zen, a drop-out from the school of the koan, what I admire and respect about Zen is that it is different. It represents the complete converse of the premises on which we proceed in the West. Unlike some other Oriental schools, especially those of Westernized Hindus, it does not claim to be "using different words for the same thing." It does not claim to incorporate all existing truths into a more all-embracing one. It picks us up and, often, throws us down because it cannot and will not be assimilated into our normal ways of thinking.

Because Zen is so different, it is a kind of giant koan itself. The thousands of little koans it uses, such as the one I meditated on, point beyond themselves to the ultimate koan. Zen itself is the sound of one hand clapping. This is why I resist well-intentioned Western efforts to explain or assimilate Zen. The late Thomas Merton made strenuous efforts, especially in the latter years of his life, to identify certain Zen words and practices with those of the Desert Fathers or other parts of the Western contemplative tradition. But the more Merton attempts to equate the Oriental *prajna* with the *logos* of the Greek fathers, or the *sunyata* of the Zen with the *todo y nada* of St. John of the Cross, the more unconvincing he becomes, especially when he concludes with the assertion that all Zen really needs to bring it to completion is "the Risen and Deathless Christ."

I'm afraid I hear the golden laughter again. Zen is not just an incomplete or culturally conditioned Oriental version of something Christianity teaches better or more comprehensively. Even though some Zen writers themselves try at times to minimize the differences, it is important *how* they do it. Zen writers do not proceed by examining the two traditions and noting alleged similarities, as Merton does. Rather, they minimize differences by denying, on the basis of Zen logic, that the whole idea of "difference" has any validity, no matter what it is applied to. Since ultimately nothing is different from anything else, why should Zen and Christianity differ? The ironic outcome of all this is that although some Christian and some Zen writers can agree that there are no important differences between the two traditions, they do so on the basis of premises which are so contradictory that they reveal the difference more starkly than ever.

The importance of Zen is that it cannot be accommodated to Western ways of thought and living. No matter how it is sliced or packaged, its singularity cannot be hidden. Despite what Zen teachers help their students to do in learning to glimpse an inclusive void or to realize a detached tranquility, Zen practice inevitably produces jarring differences and difficult choices. R. C. Zaehner, the great Catholic scholar of Oriental thought, has written that Zen is a spirituality for men and women "before the fall." He may be right. Zen resolutely holds to a vision which deals with pain, desire, choice, loss and tragedy in such a way that, while it does not deny their reality, it does not affirm it either ("neither affirming nor denying"). It equates work and play, doing and non-doing, rest and movement, being and non-being. It is a spirituality for saints and innocents, and insofar as all of us sinners maintain at least a memory or an intuition of that innocence, Zen will always have an appeal. The trouble is that most of us live "after the fall," and, if that is true, a mode of existence based on innocence can become both a temptation and a torture. Most of us need a religion for sinners.

By "fall" I do not mean an antediluvian transgression by some remote forefather; and by "sinners" I do not mean taboo breakers or even moral incompetents. To say we live in a "fallen world" means that we find ourselves in a cosmos where that primal unity that Zen allows us to glimpse is broken. It is broken, furthermore, not just because something is askew in our perception of it, but because something is askew in the thing itself. The whole creation "groans in travail," writhing and changing, heading either for a new black hole or an as yet unimagined new stage. Christianity postulates an integral link between the human phenomenon and the rest of the creation. It teaches that human beings are somehow both the victims and the perpetrators of this strange askewness. We suffer from the creation's brokenness and we often make it worse.

This underlying philosophical difference goes a long way toward explaining the messy unevenness of a lot of Christian art and liturgy, as contrasted with the striking balance, symmetry and order of Zen art. Zen has neither confessions nor Te Deum's, neither transgression nor transfiguration. Christianity is fascinated with hell and heaven. It plunges deeper and leaps higher. But at its heart, Christianity retains the hope that amidst death and suffering something is changing, not just in me but in reality itself. All this means that our liberation lies not just in altering our perception, as Zen would have it, but in opening ourselves to a cosmic energy which is overcoming desolation and pain.

Zen students sometimes claim that it is Zen which really goes deeper, since it sees beyond the *apparent* ups and downs to a common void beneath. They may be right. I am not arguing that the Christian vision is more accurate or even more credible —only that it is different. I came away from my joust with Zen bruised, humbled and, I hope, a little wiser. I also came away knowing that I had touched the outer edge of something *other* than anything I had ever known before. And Zen, despite my "failure," had taught me a lesson my further forays were to confirm—that once one starts down the road of "participation," almost anything can happen

3 The Flesh of the Gods: Turning On and Turning East

During a visit in 1973 to San Francisco, another thriving neo-Oriental center, I noticed a curious sign outside the Hare Krishna temple there. It read: STAY HIGH ALL THE TIME! CHANT TO KRISHNA! I remembered that sign when two young followers of the Maharaj Ji told me with enthusiasm that since they had "received the knowledge" from one of his mahatmas, they no longer used any drugs at all. "We have something a thousand times better," they said.

Plainly, one issue I eventually had to face in my study of neo-Oriental movements was the question of whether the tide of Eastern spirituality in the 1970s was the successor of the psychedelic upsurge of the 1960s. Many of the young devotees I talked to in Cambridge thought it was, and offered their own experience as evidence. Some saw their movement from LSD to Eastern religion as a conversion from confusion and self-destruction to clarity and health. Others saw it as a natural progression from one level of discovery to another. In nearly every neo-Oriental movement I had studied, the use of drugs was strictly forbidden. What intrigued me in particular was the frequent assertion by people who had taken psychedelic drugs that their drug experience sharply undercut the credibility of any form of "Western" faith-vision and made some sort of "Eastern" religious world view the only credible one. Did the present "Turn East" of the seventies emerge from the turn-on of the sixties?

I was not experientially prepared for this part of my study, in part because my own relationships to psychedelic drugs had been strangely out of phase. I was a graduate student at Harvard during the years when Timothy Leary and Richard Alpert (who later changed his name to Baba Ram Dass) were engaged there in their early, controversial research on the effects of ingesting psilocybin and LSD. Reports about their discoveries were whispered through Harvard Yard, but at that time there was little of the cultic or counterculture overtones that were later attached to the word "psychedelic." Still, there was excitement. I remember a scholarly senior professor of religion stopping me once on Kirkland Street in the midst of a pelting rain to describe his delight when he first listened to Bach's B Minor Mass after swallowing a small dose of a newly discovered substance he thought was called "LS-Something," administered by a young psychology teacher named Timothy Leary. As I felt the water seeping through my clothes, he went on to tell me that Leary was doing some promising research in the use of this drug at the Concord State Reformatory.

I was drenched but unimpressed. My first direct contact with Leary occurred a few weeks later. He had become puzzled by the religious images the prison inmates invariably used in describing an LSD trip. Looking for clues, he came to the Divinity School and asked me and some other doctoral students if we would like to try it. Leary argued, quite plausibly, that if scholars in the religious field could experience LSD, they might help him (at that time he described himself as "nonreligious") to understand why his prison subjects talked so frequently about "heaven and hell" or "seeing God" or "being born again" after taking the drug.

It sounded sensible, and it would certainly have been a change from sitting at a desk in the stacks at Widener Library. But I declined. I was eager to get out of school and preoccupied with completing my general examinations while trying to hold down a full-time job. Besides, I was suspicious of any kind of drug. I hesitated even to take aspirin or No-Doz, and I was reluctant to entrust my mind to some newly discovered pharmacological unguent. The Bach I listened to sounded pretty good already. Nor was my theological stance at the time particularly open to the exploration of ecstatic visions, religious or otherwise. I was a disciple of Dietrich Bonhoeffer's "religionless Christianity" and a strong believer in the Protestant neo-orthodox suspicion of all forms of "subjectivism"; so I doubted that Leary's special sugar cubes were going to contribute much to the ending of the Cold War, the abolition of segregation or the building of a nonacquisitive society.

Also, I was just plain scared. I had sometimes secretly wondered whether my toehold on sanity, already buffeted by years of graduate study, was as secure as it appeared to my friends; and I vaguely sensed that there were some remote closets of my inner self I would prefer not to open.

I became even more unwilling to take part in LSD experiments when my closest friend among the graduate students, a witty and imaginative man, became, temporarily at least, a kind of LSD convert and evangelist. Before his first "trip" we sometimes would sit for hours in Harvard Square cafés talking about everything from Greek mythology to modern philosophical ethics. Suddenly he wanted to talk about nothing but LSD: *The Magic Mountain* was a trip; the *Iliad* was a trip; *The Divine Comedy* was a trip. My incredulity bothered him and my reluctance to swallow the magic pill raised a barrier between us. The more he wheedled, the more I resisted, until gradually we began to avoid each other. I blamed Leary and acid for sabotaging a rare friendship.

I left Harvard soon after Leary was dismissed. Shortly after that, LSD became an international *cause célèbre*, and also much harder to obtain. This created a problem for me. Whenever it came out at dinner parties that I had actually been at Harvard during Leary's experimentation and had *not* taken acid, people looked at me as though I had muffed the opportunity of the epoch. Even those who were strongly against drugs seemed surprised that I had missed such an unusual chance. I became apologetic and embarrassed. I eventually decided that if the occasion ever presented itself in what appeared to be reassuring circumstances, I would ingest some LSD. Ironically, such an opportunity did not come until ten years later, and my experiences with LSD were neither frightening nor terribly significant. The real vertigo of a classical psychedelic experience did not come to me on the wings of an LSD cube at all. It came, rather, during a few days I spent in March 1974 with the Huichole Indians in San Luis Potosí State in the desert wilderness north of Mexico City, and it came through those small green-gray root growths called by the Huicholes "our little deer," by the Spanish *mescalina* and by most people "peyote."

Most writers on psychedelics stress what they designate as "set" and "setting." "Set" means the mental attitude or predisposition one brings to the experience: fear, curiosity, hope or skepticism. "Setting" refers to the physical and psychological environment within which one actually ingests the substance. When I went into the desert with the Huicholes, my set was curious and hopeful. The setting was magnificent. And something quite radiant occurred.

There are only about fifteen thousand Huicholes left in all of Mexico today. Always a somewhat obscure group, though they seem to be linguistically and culturally akin to the historically more prominent Aztecs, the Huicholes maintain traditions of religion and art that are worthy of extensive study. They weave bright red and yellow fabrics, shape their own pottery and construct a unique variety of sand painting. They coax maize and lentils from the soil with primitive tools. They keep largely to themselves, rarely participating in the growing industrial-consumer culture around them. Their religion is a synthesis of Catholic processions and pre-Columbian myths. It includes Lenten penance, fasts, dances and the annual ritual slaughter of a young bull. But what interests people most about the Huicholes is that they have used peyote in their rituals for many generations.

Once a year the Huicholes, who are scattered over three or four states in tiny isolated farming communities in the mountains, delegate a contingent of forty or fifty men and women, accompanied by a few children who have reached the age for puberty rites, to leave the villages and go out into the withering desert of San Luis Potosí State to bring home a year's supply of peyote. The hundred miles they have to traverse from the villages to the desert was once relatively free of human settlements. Now the same territory is crisscrossed by highways, power lines and railway tracks. Villages and small towns have appeared, so the reserved Huicholes—whose feathered bonnets and strange language make them objects of curiosity—have looked for more and more circuitous routes. The pilgrimage became increasingly arduous. Finally a colonel in the Mexican army who had been a patron and protector of the Huicholes offered to transport them in trucks over the most heavily inhabited parts of the route. The Indians reluctantly agreed, so now rubber tires and internal-combustion engines dispatch these pretechnological folks part of the way from their wood and stone shacks to the hiding place of the sacred cactus; they are screened from the mockery of the gawkers they would otherwise encounter along the road.

I first became acquainted with the Huicholes through a Mexican psychiatrist and public health physician named Salvador Roquet whom I met while I was teaching in Mexico in the spring of 1974. Roquet is highly regarded in Mexico for his advanced work in the psychotherapeutic use both of natural psychoactive substances such as peyote cactus, jimson weed and "magic mushrooms" and of synthetic substances such as LSD. Fifteen years ago, while working as a public health official, he became interested in the possible clinical uses of folk medicines and natural hallucinogens. Roquet has now successfully treated nearly a thousand patients in his clinic in Mexico City using his own bold combination of music therapy, psychodrama, group marathon and psychoactive drugs. Growing numbers of North American and Latin American doctors who have observed his work believe he may be on the edge of a clinical breakthrough in the treatment of people suffering from mild or severe depression and other neurotic conditions.

For a number of years Roquet worked both as a psychiatrist, seeing private patients and lecturing at the university medical school, and as a public health physician combating yellow fever. While working in remote areas of Mexico he became familiar with indigenous curing and healing rites but never thought much about their possible relevance for psychotherapy. In the late 1960's, when he was working in mountainous Oaxaca State of Southern Mexico, Roquet met a legendary old woman named Maria Sabina, a *curandera,* or healing woman. Her use of the *amanita muscaria* mushroom in healing ceremonies often seemed to help her clients, and it occurred to Roquet that some of his depressed patients back in Mexico City might profit from such a prescription. When he returned to his clinic he found five patients willing to give it a try. They all traveled to Oaxaca.

The wrinkled old woman chanted, prayed, fed the patients magic mushrooms and shepherded them through a pioneering venture into their own unconscious. Afterward, Roquet noticed that each of the five patients made a pronounced leap forward in therapy. From then on, with the guidance of Maria Sabina and of other indigenous practitioners of the curing arts, he began to use the natural hallucinogens in his own treatment of patients.

Roquet was not the first modern psychiatrist to make use of psychedelic drugs in therapy. He is probably the first, however, to do his work in such close contact with "primitive" practitioners. Several times each year Roquet travels either north to the Huichole desert country or south to the forested mountains of Oaxaca to renew his acquaintance with his Indian friends. During these trips he often gathers plants to use in his own practice, and he always takes along with him some of his staff and a few of his patients as a kind of ritual reenactment of that first curing liturgy in Maria Sabina's hut. Being invited to accompany him on one of these expeditions to the Huichole country enabled me to go where only a few white Westerners have ever gone and to taste the "flesh of the gods" in a setting prepared by a thousand years of prayer and practice.

Our sortie into the Huicholes' terrain bore few of the marks of a sober scientific enterprise. It looked more like an ill-prepared summer camping trip or a family outing. Staff members from the clinic haphazardly pushed portable hi-fi equipment, medical files, sleeping bags and coffeepots into an assortment of Fiats, VWs and one American compact. Roquet took along his wife, his ten-year-old son and his two youngest children, Roberto and Sarita, who were only four and five. There were nine patients and five staff members. One patient brought his girlfriend. I came as Roquet's personal guest. The Mexican army colonel met us along the way and accompanied us for the last leg of the journey, filling us in on Huichole character and mythology as we neared the desert. He also stayed with us during the visit as a kind of interlocutor between the Huicholes and ourselves.

It was not an easy journey. We traveled by car through the night, switched to a train in the morning, disembarked in the early afternoon and then choked and swayed the last hour in an open truck on a pitted path that billowed with gray dust. When we finally arrived at their campsite, sixteen sleepless hours after our departure from Mexico City, the Huicholes did not welcome us with songs and feasting. They watched us without expression as we jumped stiffly off the truck's tailgate, coughing and wheezing, piled our boxes and blankets on the sand and looked apprehensively at the desert. Was this where we would find wisdom, locked in the stares of the Huicholes and in the cactus bushes that stretched as far as we could see in all directions? My first thought, after trying unsuccessfully to brush the granulated dust particles from my tongue and lips with an even dustier handkerchief, was "Those Indians really don't want us here, and they're right." Just then the truck driver who had brought us noisily shifted gears, wheeled the vehicle around and headed back in the direction from which we had come, where I suspected he had a warm shower and a bed waiting.

We pitched our camp like the city folks we all were by piling dead cactus in a mound and tossing our sleeping bags down around it. At the colonel's suggestion we stationed ourselves about a hundred yards from the nearest Huichole campfire. The Huicholes had separated into three small groups strung out along a half mile of rocks, sand, cactus and (I was sure) scorpions, lizards and rattlesnakes. By the time our campsite was habitable the sun was setting, and for supper we had fresh apples which we had bought in a *mercado* on the way, cold tortillas and warm Coca-Cola. I ate sitting on my lumpy sleeping bag trying ineffectually to remove the thorns and needles that had implanted themselves in my pants, shirt, socks and various parts of my person. Mario, one of the clinic's staff, sauntered by where a group of us were crouched. Speaking casually, he warned us not to wander around in the dark too much because a four-inch needle had just penetrated his leather boot. I was wearing rubber-soled tennis sneakers and I didn't have a flashlight.

But the sunset changed my mood. The enormous blazing presence that had scorched our skins all afternoon was now a tiny red ball. As it teetered toward a world's edge serrated by the misshapen fingers of black cactus trunks, it seemed to compensate for its diminished size by reaching its shriveling purple arms all around the horizon. It was almost as though it wanted to hang on for a few extra minutes, or maybe it wanted to apologize to us for the blistering ordeal of the day and to demonstrate how much we were going to miss it. It seemed to cling for a long time to the edge. Everyone stopped talking and watched. Then quickly it sank. And we started to miss it, because the night got chilly, then cold, then raw. We snuggled into our bags, taking our thistles in with us. Most of us had not slept for nearly forty-eight hours.

But we were not allowed to sleep very long. The colonel had been talking with the Huicholes in their own language since we arrived. A few hours after sunset he roused us and told us that our Indian hosts had invited us—maybe "summoned us" puts it more clearly—to undergo a ritual purification without which we could not go near the peyote, or even stay in the desert. The colonel spoke calmly, translating what seemed to be the exact, subtle phrasing of the Huichole message into well-modulated Spanish. But he was quite insistent. Even the children were to be included. We all made our way over to the nearest Huichole fire.

The Huicholes eat some of the new peyote each night while they are gathering it. As we approached their fire they were chanting and playing reed flutes and small drums, and one of them—I blinked when I saw it—was teasing intervals from an old violin. We watched and listened, squatting just outside their circle. The inmost group seemed to be composed entirely of mature men who chanted, ate pieces of peyote, and occasionally called in other men or women from the larger circle to eat the plant or drink its juice from an earthen mug. The colonel was sitting with us, listening intently, and I noticed that he was softly translating the words of the chants into Spanish for those who were near him; so I crawled behind him and listened.

Some of the chants were traditional prayers and incantations to the high god of the tribe and to his coequal consort who is believed to be the generator of all life. Some prayers were addressed to the ancestors who, though gone in body, hover nearby and sometimes materialize themselves in pieces of white quartz (which sparks brilliantly when struck at night, a sure sign of inherent life). But some of the chants were also original improvisations. These were especially interesting to me because they indicated what a Huichole Indian who has been put more directly in touch with his unconscious by the chemical effect of the mescalin in the peyote ruminates about. I strained my ears to catch the colonel's translation above the thump of the drums and the rising and falling of the chant.

What the Huicholes were chanting about was rifles and plastic water jars. They were troubled by what we would call "technology" and the damage it could wreak on their way of life. They know that technologies always exact a price, that they carry with them new attitudes and values that dramatically alter a culture. So the Huicholes wailed about metal tools and kerosene. They pleaded with the ancestors to try to understand that in spite of the great danger these new inventions brought with them, they did make life easier. They said they were sorry to have to use modern implements. I edged near and asked the colonel if they also seemed troubled about the truck that brought them here. He said no.

After about two hours the tone of the ritual changed. The confession seemed to be past. The Huicholes laughed and moved about with more animation. The drumbeats became more irregular and the flute music wilder. The violinist had moved his fingers up the fingerboard so that the notes now sounded more like pizzicato plucking, though he was still using a bow. Also, our feathered hosts now seemed to notice us more and gestured for us to come closer to the fire, which I did gladly, since my buttocks and back were beginning to feel numb with cold.

About midnight the music and chanting stopped. The fire crackled for a while and then the Huichole spokesman asked us, through the colonel, if we were now ready for the purification. We said we were. He walked to a woven bag and then came back and gave us each a short strand of yellow rope. We were instructed to sit quietly for a while and think of whatever sins or transgressions might make us unworthy to join the search for the magical little deer, the peyote. For each trespass we were to make a small knot in the rope. Afterwards we would throw our rope strands in the fire and our sins would be purged as the flames devoured the hemp.

I remember wondering at the time whether this part of the ritual had always been there or whether it had come in with the Dominicans and Franciscans during the Spanish *conquista.* Later I discovered not only that it had been there before the Spanish came but also that similar practices can be found among peoples who have never been touched by Christianity. Few cultures are without some ritual recognition that human beings can injure their appropriate relationship to a cosmic or social order and need some symbolic way of restoring it. This aspect of the Huichole ritual may come as a surprise to the sophisticated modern admirers of unspoiled primitive religion who somehow think Western faith alone contains a penitence-and-forgiveness axis.

My reflections on the sources of the ritual did not last long. With the other pilgrims from Mexico City I crouched on the sand, the jet-bright desert stars overhead, the sparks from the pyre sailing up to meet them, and thought hard about my life. I tied several knots, and when I threw the rope on the fire a little later it cheered me to see it devoured by the coals. The next day several of the people in our party told me they had felt silly at first but had found themselves swept along and cleansed by the tying and immolating. Even the children got the point and tied some knots in their smaller stringlets.

After we had thrown our transgressions into the fire, the shaman came by each of us individually, brushing us with a tuft of horsehairs and blessing us. Then we were dismissed. We were not given any peyote, since the Huicholes believed we should hunt and dig our own the next day. The ritual was over, but by now we all felt so purified and so wide-awake that we didn't want to crawl back into our bedrolls with the lizards and scorpions. Some of the staff and patients chatted and ate apples. Others of us cut through the darkness to the second Huichole campfire, where a similar ceremony was going on. We watched and listened, though without the benefit of translation.

Eventually we went to bed, but we didn't sleep long. Since the desert heat gets intolerable in the middle of the day, it is best to find the peyote in the early morning. We were awakened by the indomitable colonel and, after brief instructions by our Indian hosts, set out in small groups to find the little deer. The Huicholes had taught us how, when we found it, to intone a prayer of apology to its spirit, how to cut it carefully with special short-bladed knives so as to preserve the root, and how to dry and string it for later use.

Peyote is a root plant. It usually grows near the trunk of a larger cactus. Since only an inch or so of its top protrudes above the ground and it is never larger around than a small saucer, one of the early Spanish explorers was moved to praise it for its modesty and seemliness. But it was not hard to find, and after a few hours of searching, stopping now and then to gaze at a horizon totally clear of buildings, roads, power lines or any other evidence of human touch, we had assembled a sackful. We came back to our camp just as the sun, having lost again the soft color of the previous evening, began to simmer everything into a shiny white blur. We tried to sidle up to the larger cactus plants, close enough to be in the narrow strip of shade but far enough away to avoid the needles. Since the Coca-Cola was gone, we drank lukewarm Orange Crush, nibbled at the last of the apples, and wrapped some hard rolls around slices of sticky cheese. Some people even slept a little, but I stayed awake and thought.

As I lay on the sand, I remembered that I had not come here with any real intention of actually eating any peyote. I had come to the desert, I thought, to observe, not to participate. Perhaps I might pocket a mouthful or two of the little deer in my denim jacket pocket and gnaw on it discreetly while the patients were experiencing the divine madness. But I would not be in the inner circle.

A large desert hawk, a bird of prey, darted to a stop several hundred feet above where I lay and hovered motionless in the air. As I watched it I knew I would never be back here again, that this was a singular, perhaps unrepeatable opportunity. I turned my head and looked over toward the Huicholes. They had slung long strings of peyote cuttings on cords to dry and were lying in the cactus shade quietly talking with each other. My body, which should have been aching from sleeplessness, dust burn, thistle pricks and the bruises of a night spent sprawled on roots and pebbles, felt buoyant and fresh. I decided that if Roquet invited me, I would be a full participant in the peyote session. I looked up, and the hawk flew away. Satisfied, I balled up my jacket, placed it under my head, took a last swig of Orange Crush and went to sleep.

When I woke an hour later, the people in our group were gathering all the peyote we had cut into one batch to show our hosts. The Huicholes examined it closely and appeared to be blessing it, but I couldn't tell because the colonel didn't seem to want to translate. Then one of the high moments of the whole adventure took place. The Huicholes sat facing us, and one sensed they had become friendlier than they were when we arrived, although the outward expression on their faces was unchanged. One of them spoke.

We had come to the desert in search of the little deer, he told us. We had been purified, had sought out the magical fawn and were now ready. This little deer, he continued, had for a very long time helped his people to talk with their gods and their ancestors. (I thought I noticed that the words "god" and "ancestor" sounded similar in Huichole but I can't be sure.) He paused. They were grateful to the little deer, he said, for what it always did for them. Without it they could hardly live. But, he said suddenly furrowing his brown brow, "the gods and ancestors of the Huicholes are not your gods and ancestors." Now, he told us, we were on our own. The Huicholes could do nothing more for us. We should move our camp to a hill some two hundred yards away, and there, during the coming night and day, we should try, with the little deer's help, to talk with our own gods and our own forebears. He stopped, looked at each of us, and then turned and walked back with his companions to the fire that flickered only fifty yards away.

The new camp we created looked more like a temple than had our first one, which had resembled a bivouac of inept boy scouts. On the high ridge we dug a huge rectangular fire pit and arranged the bedding around it symmetrically. Some people dragged in piles of firewood while Roquet and his staff set up the portable hi-fi equipment through which the spirits of our gods and ancestors—Bach's B Minor Mass, Beethoven's Ninth

Symphony, Mozart's *Requiem*, Gregorian chants and a record called "The Flutes of Israel"—would sing to us all that night. As I dug and dragged and sweated, helping with the preparations, I became more and more eager not to miss my chance. Roquet noticed. "Do you want to participate," he asked me, "instead of just watching?" My answer came immediately: "*Cómo no?* Of course I do."

Seven patients, two staff members and I stayed up all that night around the fire, sang, laughed, cried and stared at the cosmic arch above us. And ate the flesh of the little deer. All the while we were carefully watched by the colonel and Dr. Roquet and his staff, who had portioned out the exact amount of peyote we each should have. The children slept in their ponchos by the fire, oblivious to the music. And from the darkness just outside our circle the Huicholes also watched us, silently, as we had watched them the night before.

The chemically active ingredient in peyote is mescalin, which is structurally related to psilocybin and LSD. Although some people call these substances "hallucinogens" (capable of triggering hallucinations) or even "psychotomimetics" (creating states of mind that seem psychotic), Roquet refuses to use this terminology, since few people really hallucinate when under the influence of these substances. They see and hear and feel what is actually there, only much more intensely. Roquet believes that the term most psychologists prefer, "psychedelic," has become relatively useless because of its sensational attachment to vivid poster art and fortissimo guitar music. In my experience, these substances suspend temporarily the feeling-inhibiting and perception-censoring mechanisms that operate in us during our "normal" hours. They do not *add* anything of their own. They are "tools" in the best sense of the word. They enable us to feel with full pungency the most deeply buried joys and fears our memories hold. They help us to see the starkness and complexity of what is around us, devoid of the gauze with which our manipulative minds usually cover them. They help us to remember past happinesses grown dim from time, present loves, bygone pains of separation and abandonment. But these substances are terribly potent. They are the psychological equivalent of nuclear energy, capable of doing enormous good and creating awesome destruction. No wonder the Huicholes wanted us to be purified before they let us touch peyote.

Peyote does not taste good. It has the stringy consistency of a turnip and the bitterness of a sour pickle. The first feeling I remember having a half hour after eating the initial slice was one of restlessness. I wanted to pace around the fire, move my arms, breathe quickly, wrinkle my nose, flex my leg muscles, perhaps trot a little. Maybe I was just cold, but it felt to me then more like impatience, a fidgety kind of wanderlust. So I walked around the fire several times, then sat.

Some of the participants gagged and retched on the pieces of peyote. But they didn't seem to mind. The Huicholes had said this might happen, that it wouldn't hurt. The little deer was cleaning us of our remaining impurities. Once one of the patients, a young Mexican film-maker named Felipe, put his arms around me and laughed hilariously because I, the sole gringo, was the only one who did not throw up. I told him not to give me too much credit too soon.

As the choral movement of the Ninth Symphony came onto our portable hi-fi, Caterina, one of the young woman patients, looked at the sky, now resplendent with a million stars, and told us she was about to give birth to the whole universe. At the time nothing seemed more sensible to me. She lay back, drew up her knees, and with the rest of us attending, grunted and moaned in travail until she had birthed all the spiral nebulae and the milky way. After the astral birth, exhausted and satisfied by her labor, Caterina told us she could now die happy. But she didn't. After a half-hour death on her bedroll she was up dancing to a Mozart *Kyrie*.

I sat by the fire, trembling, scared by the awful power of motherhood. Next to me sat a late-middle-aged patient named Maria. Who better for a mother? As my trembling continued I crawled over to her and nestled against her legs. Pulling myself into a fetal curve I pushed harder and harder between her knees, thighs and trunk. I became smaller, and though I knew I was by a fire in the central Mexican desert, I also knew I was back where I had come from, in the warm sustaining amniotic fluid that is sea and earth and mother.

Maria acted her part well. Roquet believes that in this form of therapy patients become therapists for each other, in mutual acting-out, and intense feeling expression. It is a therapeutic equivalent of the priesthood of all believers. Whether or not she was therapist or priest I don't know, but Maria was the perfect mother. She cradled her large prenate without smothering it (I am taller and heavier than she is). She crooned and soothed, but then, after several minutes, it was time to leave. I knew, and she knew too. The birth was easy, unresisted. She did not expel me, but she did not cling either. As I unwound, stood and stretched, she laughed and wordlessly rolled her head around.

Again I paced: Jason in search of the fleece, Odysseus on the high seas, the pilgrim, explorer, wanderer. The fire snapped and hissed. I listened. Flat on my stomach now, I watched it, felt its heat pulsations, listened to its flames oxydizing cactus branches. Suddenly I felt close to the animals: the snakes that live all the time on their bellies and see the whole world from this angle; the wolves and coyotes who fear the fire but creep close for warmth. I hissed, I crawled. I bared my teeth and stalked around the fire pit on all fours. I spat. I felt the warm sand around the pit against my face and the hard grains under my nails. Two of the clinic staff, always alert to the possibility of people hurting themselves, but never intrusive, got to their feet and stood behind me. The notion came to me that they thought I had flipped out and now they could be really useful psychiatric aides. I wanted to say to them, "It's OK, you can sit down again," but I was enjoying myself too much. Behind the aides I heard someone say, "It's anger!" and I wanted to snort. I had rarely been less angry.

Dr. Roquet had collected our watches before we started taking the peyote. He never likes his patients to be checking on the time because it distracts them from concentrating on what is going on inside them and around them. He removes all the props of normalcy so a patient descends into a period of temporary personality disorganization, a brief madness. The idea is that undergoing such dislocation, though it will be jarring and unsettling, reduces the obstacles to healing. A confrontation with repressed feelings occurs which might require years of treatment to reach by other techniques.

Since we had no watches, I had no idea what time it was

when one of the patients first noticed the morning star and pointed it out to us, glistening like a crown jewel over the eastern horizon. The other patients saw it and agreed it was beautiful, and then went back to whatever they were doing before. But I could not go back. In the church I belong to there is a group of young adults who like to sing selections from a nineteenth-century collection called *The Sacred Harp,* the oldest hymnbook still in use in America. They perform these old hymns with the same precision that other people devote to motets. One of the songs in this collection is a simple, stirring one entitled "Bright Morning Stars Are Rising." When I saw the morning star in the desert sky over San Luis Potosí State, I heard that hymn sung by a fifty-thousand voice choir, or so it seemed. And it was all for me.

Strong feelings often center on one concrete object. That is what makes a symbol a symbol. It becomes the receptacle or conduit for something far more than itself. That night the morning star became for me the sign of a universe that throbbed with love—not just general beneficence, but personally focused love, pouring through real people. Watching the morning star I felt more intensely than I ever had before what I have nearly always believed, and had sensed on some previous occasions: that "God is love" is not just a pious hope but a factual statement about the character of the universe. The morning star and the song about it fused. The song was the star and the star was the song.

The feeling was too strong. At first I staggered out into the desert reaching toward the morning star. Then I fell, knelt, wept and cried, stood up, fell again. My knees shook and I trembled. Twice I tried to turn back toward the fire, away from the star. But each time its power turned me around and I was drawn toward it, only to stumble and fall again. I was deliriously happy. I thought of my family and my students, neighbors and friends—all the people whose love for me is a vehicle of the vital energy of the cosmos. Finally, exhausted from crying and weak with joy, I crept back to my colleagues around the fire and lay still.

The vision was not "pantheistic." The morning star was not the *object* of my veneration. It was, to use very traditional language, "an outward and visible sign of an inward and invisible grace," the standard textbook definition of a sacrament. Was it a "mystical experience"? I don't think so. I did not lose myself or merge with the star. I did not return as a drop of water to the great ocean or soar out of my body. I knew where I was and who I was at all times. What I felt was an Other moving toward me with a power of affirmation beyond anything I had ever imagined could exist. I was glad and grateful. No theory that what happened to me was "artificially induced" or psychotic or hallucinatory can erase its mark. "The bright morning stars are rising," as the old hymn puts it, "in my soul."

A short time later a gray line appeared all along the eastern horizon. Each of us noticed it, one by one fell silent, and walked toward the eastern edge of our camp. The sun was about to rise.

The sun, of course, rises every day. We all expect it; or rather, we rarely think about it. But somehow, on this particular morning in the desert, after births and deaths, tears and cries of gladness, the sun's possible arrival seemed like a miracle beyond the telling. As we watched, I thought of the Aztecs, those ancient kinsmen of our Huichole hosts, who were so afraid the sun would not rise some day that they made a sacrifice by cutting out living human hearts every year to make sure it did. We watched quietly. The gray line widened and became lighter. Then it came, a tiny bright yellow crescent, then a half-circle: the sun, our old tormentor and friend. We cheered briefly, weakly, and then collapsed. Our night with our gods and ancestors was over. Across the ravine the Huicholes were preparing breakfast. At our fireside Roberto and Sarita sat up and scurried to the edge of the camp to urinate. Somewhere, a few hills away, a burro whinnied. Sitting on her wrinkled sleeping bag, Maria was carefully applying her mascara. A new day had begun.

During the morning we sat around the fire, smaller now and by daylight less fearsome when compared to its blazing prototype in the sky. And we talked about the night. Dr. Roquet believes that the peyote vision is not complete until each person has talked through what he or she felt, has heard the responses of the others, and has had a chance to integrate it all into the ongoing reality of quotidian life. Peyote is not magic, and if the insight it gives us remains isolated in the demiworld of a "trip," it can do more harm than good. So we talked. We spoke of Hernando's fear, of Caterina's becoming *la madre del universo,* of Maria's maternal serenity and my fetal restlessness. I tried to talk about the morning star, but it was hard to do, especially in a language that was not my own.

After lunch we said goodbye to the Huicholes and retraced our path to Mexico City. We traveled all night, and when we arrived it was Sunday morning, but the traffic was brisk, so we said awkward *Hasta luego's* as we dropped weary people at street corners and bus stops. I returned to my room in the San Angel district, and even before I had showered I sat at my tape recorder and described as much as I could of what had happened. My precautions were not all that necessary. Months later, my memory of those days and nights in the desert was as clear as ever.

My visit with the Huicholes reminded me again that the old saying, "One man's food is another's poison," still holds. For the North American counterculture of the 1960's, swept along in the compulsive quest for some experience one could truly *feel,* the psychedelics became a new thing one had to do, a stimulus for jaded senses, a "trip." For the Huicholes they are none of these. Rather, they are an essential link with ancestors and gods, a sacrament. The hippies used them to escape their culture; the Huicholes use them to enter deeper into theirs.

So there is indeed some connection between the Turn On of the sixties and the Turn East of the seventies. Both are a scream of longing for what a consumer culture cannot provide—a community of love and the capacity to experience things intensely. Both may supply temporary, short-term relief. Neither can remedy the situation very deeply or for very long. It is pointless and irrelevant to bicker either with those who need to rely on drugs or with those who find solace in neo-Oriental spirituality. Both have found something—which is always better than nothing. But neither has the answer we need so badly ourselves.

What the Huicholes have that we do not have is *not* peyote. We have it, or its rough chemical equivalents, so that is not the issue. What they have is a society which honors its own past, which does not set person against person in a ruthless race for gold, which honors sharing and nurturing, which has no interest in accumulating more than it needs.

We cannot copy the Huichole culture. But if we want to have a society in which plants and foods and trances and songs can be used for joyous human purposes, rather than as desperate getaways, then sooner or later we must lance the pustule that is poisoning everything else, the system of greed and gain that makes us all gluttons whether we want to be or not.

What did my visit with the Huicholes do to answer my original question about a possible link between psychedelic states and Oriental mysticism? It led me to suspect that the peculiar sociology of the "drug culture" of the 1960's gave it a predictable countercultural flavor, and that its "setting," not the chemical catalysts themselves, pushed its religious language in such an "Oriental" direction. The "set" of the people who used these substances was already upper bohemian, romantic and anti-Western, and this stance led them to use the most esoteric symbols available to codify their experiences. I doubt that there is anything essentially Oriental about the psychedelics. My experience with peyote was not "Oriental" in any sense, and may not even have been mystical. Rather, my vision involved creation stories, second births, and a star in the east signaling grace to people on earth—all very biblical, perhaps even "Christian."

A few weeks after the visit with the Huicholes I met a young anthropologist at a dinner party in a suburb of Mexico City. At my host's urging I told the anthropologist something about my visit with the Huicholes. He seemed interested, but informed me at once that I had made a serious mistake when I actually ate the peyote. Some anthropologists have tried for years to see what I saw, he said. If I had remained an observer throughout, I might have written a publishable article on the subject. But since I had not been myself all that night, what I wrote now would naturally be read with considerable suspicion.

After the anthropologist and I had parted, I thought of Dr. Roquet's question to me on the night we feasted on the little deer. Did I want to watch or to take part? I knew that the

Huicholes had brought me to the end of Phase Two of my work. I was now ready for a new level of participation in the movements I had been studying. A few weeks later I packed and left Mexico to go to the Naropa Institute in Boulder, Colorado. It was there that Phase Three really began.

4 The Hag of Naropa

The red-and-orange cushion under me felt harder than it had an hour before. The room was hot, and outside the large windows of the Karma Dzong meditation hall the increasingly loud grinding of gears and bleep of horns reminded me that Boulder's late-afternoon traffic was already in the streets. Across from me and beside me sat long rows of fellow meditators, legs crossed, eyes looking straight ahead. Some of the men had removed their shirts, but most people were dressed in jeans and tank tops or T-shirts. A lazy August fly buzzed past my nose but decided not to land. Inside me a parade of images and memories marched by, but as I noticed them I kept returning to take note of my departing breath, as the instructor had told me. I was serene and unhurried even though I had a supper engagement and the traffic noises were telling me it was time to go.

Now the horns and engines grew more insistent. I shifted my weight on the cushion and felt the familiar tiny abdominal quiver which, like a doctor's pocket bleeper, dependably reminds one of an impending obligation to be met. Instinctively I started to glance at my watch, to check on whether it was indeed time now to leave the meditation hall and join my friends for dinner. But for some reason, I did not move. I did not turn my watch toward me. I did not move my eyes toward its dial. I sat still, and slowly noticed a slight—an ever so slight—shift in my perspective. The shift was both tiny and tremendous, like the split second just before and just after midnight on New Year's Eve. At the moment when I did not look at my watch, I became aware that whether I got to supper late, or at all, was significant, but not urgent. I would go when I was ready. The choice of when and whether to go was mine. To anyone else, such a realization might seem utterly commonplace. But to me the change it signaled—not just in my attitude toward the meditation I had been trying so hard to learn, but also in my attitude toward many other things—was immeasurable. Slowly, still without looking at the watch, I slipped it off my wrist and into my pocket.

After a few minutes I glanced around at the other meditators and felt another change. They all looked the same, but somehow they also looked completely different. What had changed was that now my status was different. I was no longer merely a visitor—or a sympathetic observer or a friendly outsider. Although I did not know the names of most of the people in the hall, I felt closer to them, at least at that moment, than I did to the people outside the window scurrying to their supper-hour engagements.

The feeling left as quickly as it came. Then I did consult my watch, put my sandals on, puffed up my cushion for the next user and made my way out of the hall. On the street, too, surprisingly, I was also at home. I looked forward to supper, to seeing my friends, to conversation. I did not feel that I had been interrupted. As I walked toward the bus stop, however, I knew that on this day the meditation I had been learning for the past three weeks was no longer merely an option or a luxury. I was now a practitioner of meditation, not merely an observer. Noiselessly, almost without noticing it, I had taken another step in my journey to the East. Without being converted or changing my theology or joining anything, I had become something of an East Turner myself. Phase Three was beginning.

Perhaps, in retrospect, there was no reason to be surprised. My sympathetic trek through America's neo-Oriental county fair had been proceeding on schedule and I had been savoring all the sights. I had met fascinating people, sampled varieties of cotton fluff and candied apples, peered into the dark sideshows and listened to the spiels of the barkers. My notebooks were crammed and my collection of tapes was piling up. I knew there was a book to be written on this. Then, on this summer day in Boulder, in the middle of the midway, something I should have anticipated happened. I became a part of what I was studying.

The tourist-pilgrim had become more pilgrim than tourist. The East Turners became "us" instead of "them." The subtle line between writing about other people, with whose search I could often identify, versus writing about myself as one of the seekers, had been crossed. I was now writing about a phenomenon I was part of, and my evaluations and criticisms would now be judgments about myself.

This unexpected role reversal did not make me any less critical of many facets of the Turn East. In fact, if anything, it sharpened my awareness of the overlaid tiers of phoniness and gimmickry, of desperate need and cheap comfort which can be found in so much of the neo-Oriental mystique. But I could see the other side more clearly, too. I could detect the sources of the Turn East—the search for friends, the thirst for immediacy, in myself as well as in others. I could taste the lure of the exotic and sense the strong appeal of a teacher who knew something I wanted to know. I did not renounce any previous memberships, undergo any initiation rites or subscribe to any neo-Oriental mythology. But I did discover a *practice* which had become important, not for my study but for me. So I had to admit that, even according to my own categories, I was an East Turner myself.

It all started innocently enough. I had come to Boulder from Mexico in response to what seemed a golden opportunity to gather more impressions for my book. The opportunity came in the form of an invitation to teach a course in Christianity at the Naropa Institute, a Buddhist study center (now a college) in Boulder, which had been founded a year or two before by Chogyam Trungpa Rinpoche, who, besides being a meditation teacher, is also a scholar of Western and Buddhist art. Trungpa (the "Rinpoche" is a traditional title applied to lamas) and thousands of other Tibetans had been forced to leave Tibet in 1961 when the Chinese invaded and closed the monasteries. He first stayed in India, where many of the refugee Tibetans still live, then moved to England, studied at Oxford University, and later organized a Buddhist meditation center in Scotland. Trungpa came to the United States in 1970 and founded a meditation center called Karmê Chöling (formerly Tail of the

Tiger) in Barnet, Vermont. Then, in 1973, he started a study institute in Boulder and named it Naropa after a revered eleventh-century Buddhist teacher. In keeping with the ancient Buddhist monastic practice of welcoming visitors from the other great traditions, and also because he wants Naropa to become a genuine East-West exchange center, Trungpa invited me to teach a course on the life and teachings of Jesus there during the summer session.

It is not hard to see why a refugee lama from Tibet might settle in Colorado. The foothills of the Rocky Mountains begin at Boulder and the peaks themselves can be seen from the streets. Snow-patched cliffs and cold glens alternate with carpets of sturdy grass and mountain laurel. Steep trails and narrow valley roads climb and intersect. The air is clean and clear. The scenery probably comes closer to the Tibetan Himalayas than anything else America offers.

When I arrived at Naropa to teach my course on the New Testament, nothing in the environment surprised me. Boulder is the home of the University of Colorado. It is full of bookstores, natural-food restaurants, denim cut-offs and shoulder bags. I was at home. Also, I had taught at summer institutes before, and this one seemed familiar. There were nearly a thousand students and a faculty of forty offering almost a hundred courses. There was the usual gossip about which teachers and seminars were worth taking, where to eat, what mountain roads to explore, where the action was. Yet under the frivolity and humor and sunbathing at the pools I sensed a serious, at times frighteningly serious, commitment to the "practice," the word the Naropa students invariably applied to sitting in meditation in a regular, disciplined way. Nearly all the faculty and most of the students engaged in this "sitting" one or two hours every day, either in their own rooms or in one of the group meditation halls. And every other week many of them participated in the Sunday *nyinthun*—twelve hours of consecutive sitting with breaks only for short meals and even shorter periods of "walking meditation" around the inside of the hall. I got the message. If I was going to learn anything at Naropa I would have to "sit," and sit a lot. Furthermore, I decided I would not use a do-it-yourself approach as I had with Zen, but would take advantage of the instruction in meditation that Naropa offered.

The Tibetan method of meditating is so simple that it sounds trite. There is little emphasis on correct posture or hand position. No special clothing or setting is needed (though I found it better to wear loose clothes and to meditate in the same room with other meditators). No koans or mantras are used, at least in the early stages. No master ever hits a student with a fan. What is emphasized, however, is sitting frequently, sitting regularly, and sitting for long periods. Although many Zen instructors start their students out on short sittings and do not encourage day-long periods of meditation until the novice has learned the basics well, Trungpa seems to have enormous confidence in what sitting itself can do for those who will simply plunge in, with periodic help from an instructor. He believes that no amount of reading about Buddhist teaching will make any sense at all unless the student is engaged in sitting meditation. One night at a public lecture he shocked some experienced sitters by inviting, even urging, all eight hundred people present, many of whom were visitors who had never sat for even an hour, to participate in an upcoming twelve-hour *nyinthun.* "You can do it," he assured them, and many did.

In my own desultory attempt to learn meditation, I had already sparred with a form of Zen, using a koan—and had lost. Later I had evolved my own hybrid brand of meditation and practiced it sporadically, always realizing that something was missing when I neglected it. But I was always too busy and too undisciplined to sit regularly. At Naropa, however, I found myself in an atmosphere where sitting was somehow expected. So I picked out a red-and-orange cushion at the Pearl Street Karma Dzong in Boulder, the local branch of Trungpa's growing network of Dharmadatus (teaching and meditation centers). There I sat an hour every day, sometimes twice a day, in a sunny room with a varnished floor where from eight to eighty other meditators might gather. Most important of all, I had an instructor.

At first the only thing my instructor in the Tibetan form of meditation showed me was how to be aware of my exhaling, to "follow my breath" out into the world, identifying as far as possible with breathing out and letting go, not thinking at all about breathing in. Surprisingly I found that within a few days I had mastered the basics. Thoughts of all kinds do occur, of course, but the meditator, as in Zen, makes no effort to sort, censor or exclude. One merely returns again and again to the departing breath as a kind of home plate or ground zero. Squatting on a cushion, hands resting lightly on one's knees, eyes open but slightly lidded and not focused on anything in particular, the meditator gradually discovers a perspective on the endless rush of mental processes. It feels a bit like standing on a bridge and watching the leaves and twigs float by on the stream passing underneath. Sometimes the mind does follow one of these bits of flotsam, frequently even becoming absorbed or agitated by it. But when the meditator notices that this has happened, he or she simply returns to the departing breath again. The stream rolls on and the flotsam slowly drifts around the bend as more appears upstream.

Before I arrived at Naropa I decided I would enroll in some formal courses in Buddhism, since my previous exposure to Buddhist thought had been minimal. The catalog was crammed with intriguing seminars on the Bardo Thodol, Vajrayana literature and Theravadan theory and practice. However, since as a concept-oriented person I would be inclined to burrow in a library and read all the texts and monographs I could find on the subject, I decided—as a corrective—that this time I would approach things differently. I would go the *visual* route. So, in addition to the daily meditation with the instructor's guidance, I signed up for two courses in the history and significance of Buddhist art, one offered by Trungpa himself. I laid aside words for pictures and postures.

As the days and weeks went by, I found that although I was fascinated by the art history of Buddhism, it remained somewhat exotic and merely "interesting" for me. The meditation, however, was something else. From the very outset, from the first hour-long sitting, I sensed that something unusual was happening to me. My level of internal chatter went down. I did not invest situations with so many false hopes and fantasies. I walked away from the sitting feeling unruffled and clear-headed. I could teach with more precision and listen to people more attentively. Soon the hour or two of sitting was not a chore but something I looked forward to. I began to sense in myself something many East Turners had told me about in words I had not comprehended. Even the excited testimonies of the Divine Light people and the practitioners of Transcendental Meditation now seemed a little more credible.

Ironically, the more I meditated, following my Buddhist instructor's advice, the more my assigned role as resident Christian theologian at Naropa seemed eminently sensible and right. I even noticed certain "buddhistic" elements in Jesus that I had never seen so clearly before, especially his refusal to be what people expected him to be, his unwillingness to be drawn into abstract discussions, and his constant insistence that if people would only look closely at what was going on in their midst they would see that the Kingdom of God was already coming to them. Paradoxically my plunge into Buddhism at Naropa had made me feel more "Christian" than I had felt when I arrived there.

I found Chogyam Trungpa Rinpoche, the founder of Naropa, a likeable and approachable figure, not at all the costumed sadhu so many East Turners yearn for. He dresses in conventional Western style, with jacket and tie, forgoing all the flimflam of Guru-dom. Though many of his students want to press him into the holy man role, Trungpa constantly warns them against it. In his public lectures he pokes fun at those who are seduced by brocades and incense and exotic music. "My lineage is really quite dull," he insists. His book *Cutting Through Spiritual Materialism* sounds the same cautionary note again and again. He once warned an audience of eager listeners they should not look to him or Tibet or Buddhism for answers, that all would come clear if they could once really see the mountains outside Boulder.

Dull lineage or not, Chogyam Trungpa, in his public lectures given every Tuesday and Thursday evening, provided the big occasions of the week for everyone at Naropa. Scheduled for eight o'clock, the lectures rarely began before nine thirty, sometimes not until ten or ten thirty. Although people complained at first, they quickly learned to accept and even appreciate the teacher's tardiness. Part of the ease of adjustment was due to the physical setting. The lectures were held in the rented gymnasium of a local parochial school. The gym floor had been temporarily covered with a huge segmented rug. There were no chairs; the audience had to lie or sit on the floor. Consequently the atmosphere between eight and ten resembled a friendly beach scene. People lounged on blankets and cushions, read, chatted in small groups, snoozed, and circulated to check on friends and to gossip. No one ever seemed bored. It occurred to me that in arriving two hours late, Trungpa, who constantly criticizes the frantic pace and needless hurry of American life, had cleverly created a small oasis in time. It was a social hour without agenda, an open clearing for quiet conversation and relaxed camaraderie.

The lectures themselves were puzzling to me, at least at first. A small unimpressive brown-skinned man with a slight limp, Trungpa talks in a flat, husky voice and is often repetitious. He sits as he speaks, sips sake from a glass, indulges in long pauses, and appears to use no notes at all. At first I simply could not understand why eight hundred people would wait two hours to listen to his often tedious utterances. But as I returned each time and let his remarks connect with the realization that was slowly dawning on me while "sitting," I began to appreciate what was going on: he was using the lecture to help us grasp what was happening to us in our meditation. The lectures were a massive, if subtle, attempt to help us deal with the self-confrontation "sitting" inevitably produces.

Trungpa is a different kind of teacher from those most of us have met. Some teachers write so well one doesn't need to know them personally at all. Their printed words speak for themselves. Others teach by communicating some elusive aspect of their own person: eye contact and body movement say all. Their words mean nothing on a printed page, and little even on a tape. Still others communicate only if both teacher and student are sharing in some common enterprise. This is the way masters work with apprentices in many of the arts and crafts. Trungpa's teaching falls in the third category. His books, though interesting, are hardly commanding. When he lectures to ordinary audiences he may or may not impress his hearers, depending largely on the circumstances. But in a master-apprentice setting, where nearly everyone is working at the development of a personally adequate spiritual discipline, and where everyone knows that Trungpa, whatever his weakness, is an acknowledged master of just such a discipline, intense and genuine learning occurs. I know because I learned.

I learned so quickly at Naropa that it raised questions in my mind about the virtual disappearance of the master-apprentice axis in American higher education. Even in religious studies we generally think of fields and areas of competence. We blithely accept the divorce between a student's mastery of the subject matter and his or her personal growth and maturation. We sometimes even purposely arrange curricula to minimize the chances of a student's working too closely with any one teacher, and we tend to discourage anyone's having "disciples." While this educational strategy may facilitate the student's achieving a certain abstract competence, it perpetuates a chasm between knowing and doing, information and growth. This hiatus is not only debilitating to the student, it actually falsifies what most religious traditions teach: that mere data gathering undermines the life of faith. What happened to me at Naropa occurred not because I had learned something *about* Buddhism, but because Trungpa and his students had taught me *how* to meditate.

For me, meditation is not a mystical experience. It is almost the opposite. It forces me to pare back daydreams, cut through rosy expectations and look carefully, often even painfully, at what is actually there in front of me and inside me. There are hundreds of ways to meditate, and endless theories about what it does or doesn't do, and why. Researchers have measured the pulse, skin temperature, brain waves, and breathing rates of various people doing different kinds of meditation. They know the effects are not just mental. Many doctors, including my Harvard colleague Dr. Herbert Bensen, a cardiologist, believe, with excellent evidence, that meditation can help patients with chronic heart problems.

My own experience, mainly gained from the type of meditation I learned from Trungpa and his students, is that, far from luring me away from active participation in the world (as some critics claim it does), it enables me to think and act more decisively, to see things and people in sharper focus, and to suffer fewer regrets and recriminations. I came away from Naropa convinced that a sitting-type meditation is perfectly compatible with Christian life. Eventually it might even provide a modern equivalent of something we have lost from our heritage, the idea of a Sabbath or a stated time to cease, to do nothing, to allow what is to be. I will return to the idea in the next chapter.

Despite the fact that Naropa produced a role change in my study of the Turn East, it did not in any way lessen my doubts and suspicions about the neo-Oriental wave. It confirmed all my worst fears about how even the most valuable teaching, including the art of meditation, can be misused, often unconsciously. New adepts strode about the streets of Boulder wearing imported "meditation pants" and ostentatiously lugging their sitting cushions under their arms. Peddlers hawked vaguely Tibetan-looking bracelets and ornaments. The question of how long one had been "sitting"—and even how long one could sit at a stretch—sometimes became the arena for a sort of spiritual one-upmanship, reminding me of the way young civil rights workers used to compare the length of their jail terms in the sixties. Worst of all, I found people leaping into the labyrinth of Buddhist concepts and ill-digested Sanskrit or Tibetan terms in what often sounded like an unintended caricature of serious discipleship. Phrases like "bad karma" and "more evolved person" swirled like incense smoke screens over meals and conversations. I am sure it all made the Buddha chuckle.

My principal reservation about the Buddhist teaching I heard at Naropa, as opposed to the sitting practice itself, is that despite its explicit emphasis on not trying too hard, it seems to lay out a very long path. One hears a lot about "cessation," but there hovers in the background the specter of a stupendous mountain the seeker must eventually climb in order to become enlightened. The "path" has many stages. And to an outsider it appears cluttered with snares and laden with possibilities for backsliding and frustration. More "advanced" students hinted seductively about what lay ahead for beginners, especially in the sexual imagery of Tantra. Others talked evasively about the "hundred thousand prostrations" one must do at a certain stage, and of complex forms of visual meditation and internal chanting and the rest. Novices listened, wide-eyed, while veteran meditators smiled at their enthusiasm and looked at each other knowingly.

When I noticed all this I shuddered. It called to mind the story of the pious young Martin Luther crawling up the stairs of St. Peter's on his knees, or the practice of adding up "Hail Mary's" and "Our Father's" which eventually enraged so many Catholics. I detected in this excessive elaboration that Buddhism, like every other spiritual tradition, has an uncanny capacity to complicate the simple, to escalate an elemental insight into a colossal caricature of itself.

But the sitting meditation remains the core. No teaching should be discarded either because of the excesses of its students or the pretentiousness of its interpreters. Learning to meditate does not entail ingesting the entire corpus of Buddhist ideology, doctrine and world view—or any of it. In fact, I believe there is no reason why it cannot become an integral part of Christian discipleship. I returned from Naropa convinced that it would be a part of mine.

On the night before I left Boulder some students and faculty colleagues gave me a farewell party. During the festivities someone pressed into my hand a small book describing the life of the original Naropa, the eleventh-century sage after whom the institute had been named. On the plane the next day I pulled it out of my pocket and thumbed through the story. Naropa, it seems, was a famous Indian teacher who, by the time he had reached middle age, was the acknowledged authority in the Buddhist scriptures. In all the world he had no equal in his scholarly acumen, and students came in from far and wide to sit at his feet. One day, however, there appeared at his hut a blemished and crotchety old hag who began to berate and insult him. As he tried to study she continually taunted him and asked him about the meaning of passages in the sacred texts. Whenever he answered she merely cackled. Sometimes she would sneak up close and poke him with a stick. Finally, in a fury, Naropa shouted at her to go away and reminded her that in the entire world there was no one who was more versed in explaining the sense of the texts. The hag laughed uproariously. "Yes, you know the sense," she croaked, "you know the sense. But do you know the *meaning?*" She disappeared. And Naropa left his desk, went to the forest and apprenticed himself to a teacher. Having spent his life mastering the texts, he now wanted to learn what they meant for Naropa.

5 Meditation and Sabbath

Even before I left Tibet-in-the-Rockies for Benares-on-the-Charles, I began to wrestle with what it means to be a Christian who practices a "Buddhist" form of meditation. For many people this would not pose any problems, because mixing assorted tidbits from different religious traditions comes easily to some. But it does not come easily to me. Others would simply sever previous affiliations, but I had not done that, either. I was not a convert, and had no intention of becoming one. So the question remained: What role can meditation play in the life of a person who is neither a Buddhist nor a syncretist, but remains a Jew or a Christian?

For the past several years, Eastern meditation has been finding a larger and larger place in Christian practice. In monasteries from Maine to New Mexico, Roman Catholic contemplative orders have begun to integrate one or another form of sitting into their daily liturgical schedule. The Benedictine monks I visited in Vermont last winter began the day by "sitting" at 4:30 A.M., two hours before dawn, using cushions and postures similar to the ones I had encountered at Naropa. And in many churches, basic meditation techniques are taught to Christians, most of whom have no interest in becoming Hindus or Buddhists.

It should come as no surprise that certain Oriental spiritual disciplines are finding a resonance in the modern West. Christianity has its own contemplative tradition, much of which is highly reminiscent of such Oriental practices as sitting, breath concentration and mantra chanting. According to the New Testament, Jesus himself, despite his turbulent life, often took out times to withdraw and be alone. The early desert fathers developed a wide range of contemplative techniques. In the Eastern Christian church, a practice known as "Hesychasm," the attempt to achieve "divine quietness"—for which the Greek word is *hesychia*—emerged. One of its early proponents, St. John Climacus, taught his followers to concentrate on each breath they took, using the name of Jesus as a kind of mantra to accompany this breathing. A later Hesychast, St. Nicephorus, instructed his disciples to attach a prayer to each breath and to focus their attention on the centers of their own bodies while meditating. Later Hesychasts believed that while in such a state of prayerful contemplation people could see the inner light of the Transfiguration. This will all sound familiar to any Westerner who has recently had instruction in a form of Oriental meditation in which breath concentration, chanting or an inner light play an important role.

Christian contemplative practices in the West developed in a somewhat more intellectual and moralistic direction. St. Ignatius Loyola, the founder of the Jesuit order, prescribed a rigorous form of spiritual discipline suitable for a soldier in Christ's army. Yet even the Ignatian *Spiritual Exercises* outline methods of introspection and patterned imagining which would seem familiar to practitioners of Oriental forms. Among Protestants, the practice of daily prayer and Bible reading was once held to be indispensable to Christian life. But the failure of most churches actually to teach people how to pray and the difficulties involved in learning the difference between reading, studying and meditation on a text have produced a generation of Protestants who live with practically no spiritual discipline at all.

Still, despite similarities with Western practices, a vague uneasiness often bothers many Christians and Jews who meditate. Some feel uneasy because they seem to be filching someone else's spiritual inheritance. They suspect that to use the technique without the religious world view that comes with it is somehow dishonest, that it shows a disrespect for the whole philosophical structure within which meditational practices have come to the West. I respect the reservations these people have, and their reluctance. They are rightly suspicious of the groups that have cut meditation out of its metaphysical setting and reduced it to a mere psychological gimmick. They can not accept the world view within which meditation has been integrated in Buddhism. Yet they have found that the practice of meditation undeniably resonates with something within them. What can they do?

I have come to believe that the answer to this question lies neither in swallowing the entire corpus of Buddhist philosophy nor in reducing meditation to a psychological self-help device. Rather, a third possibility presents itself. It consists in combining the serious practice of meditation with a patient rethinking of the biblical tradition and the history of Jewish and Christian spirituality—uncovering those points in our own spiritual tradition where the functional equivalents of meditation appear. I think there are many such points—that meditation need not be viewed as an exotic import, but as something with roots in our own tradition.

I did not come to this conclusion easily, and as usual the basic insight—that Judeo-Christian spirituality has its own equivalent of the meditational practice—came to me first not from a book but through an experience that altered my way of thinking out the issue.

A few days before I was scheduled to leave Naropa, a rabbi who lives in a small town near Boulder invited me to join him and his tiny congregation in celebrating the weekly Sabbath—not just the religious service that took place in his back yard, but a genuine, old-fashioned Shabbat, a whole day of doing very little, enjoying the creation as it is, appreciating the world rather than fixing it up. I accepted the invitation and joined in the relaxed Sabbath, which lasted, as tradition dictates, from Friday sundown until sundown on Saturday. During those luminous hours, as we talked quietly, slept, ate, repeated the ancient Hebrew prayers and savored just being, rather than doing, it occurred to me that meditation is in essence a kind of miniature Sabbath. For twentieth-century Christians, and for many Jews as well, it provides a modern equivalent of what the observance of Sabbath once did, but does no more.

The Jews did not invent the idea of Sabbath. Though its origins remain obscure, it undoubtedly had antecedents in the religious milieu of the ancient Near East. It is not impossible that the core insight from which Sabbath developed is identical with the one which, under different historical circumstances, eventually produced the practice of meditation. Both prescribe a regular time when human beings *do nothing*. This connection becomes even more evident when we realize that the word for Sabbath in Hebrew comes from a root meaning "to desist." Sabbath originally meant a time that was designated for ceasing all activity and simply acknowledging the goodness of creation. It was not, at first, a day for cultic acts or long worship services. It was a time set aside for affirming what is.

But meditation and Sabbath also differ, at least when we compare Sabbath with the theories of meditation as they are now frequently taught by neo-Oriental masters. Meditation, though it begins as something one does at a particular stated time, is also often interpreted as the key to a total way of life. Sabbath, on the other hand, is one day out of seven. It never becomes a complete way of life. It represents the Israelites' recognition that although human beings can catch a glimpse of the pure realm of unity and innocence, they also live in the fractured world of division, greed and sorrow. Sabbath is Israel's ingenious attempt to live both in history and beyond it, both in time and eternity.

In the earliest recorded expression of the idea of Sabbath, in the Fourth Commandment of Moses, one day in every seven is set aside.

> Six days shalt thou labor and do all thy work; but the seventh is the Sabbath of Yahweh: in it thou shalt not do any work, thou, nor thy son, nor thy daughter, thy manservant nor thy maidservant, nor thy cattle, nor thy stranger that is within thy gates; for in six days Yahweh made heaven and earth, the sea and all that in them is, and rested the seventh day; wherefore Yahweh blessed the sabbath day and hallowed it.

At first reading, the suggestion that God "rested" after the toil of creation—the image is of a craftsman sitting down and wiping his brow—sounds quaintly anthropomorphic. The word "rest" literally means "to catch one's breath." God, like us, gets tired and has to restore himself. The passage may indeed depict a less exalted view of God than later emerges in Jewish faith. On further reflection, however, and with the anthropomorphic symbol somewhat decoded, a deeper truth appears, and with it a possible link with the tradition of sitting meditation.

The first thing to notice about God's activity on the Sabbath is that it focuses on breathing. We all stop to draw breath after we have been exerting ourselves, and the passage may mean no more than this. But to depict God himself as one who ceases work and does nothing but breathe could suggest a deeper and older stratum of spiritual consciousness which lies behind the passage itself. Breath is a source of renewal, and God, like human beings, returns periodically to the source.

The second facet of this ancient passage is even more telling Sabbath is the Jewish answer to the profound question all religions face about the relationship between doing and being, between what Indian mystics call *sat* (perfect being) and *prana* (spirit and energy). All religions must cope with the apparent contradiction between a vision of reality as ultimately changless and one that contains contrast, opposition and change. In the Bible the key terms are not "being" and "energy" but "creation" and "rest." Viewed in this light, the idea of Sabbath is not naïve or primitive at all. It is a highly sophisticated philosophical notion. It postulates an ultimate force in the universe which is not just passive and changeless but which acts and is acted upon. Yet it affirms what most religions also say about the ultimate: it is eternal and perfect. Sabbath links God and world and human beings in a dialectic of action and rest, of purposeful doing and "just sitting." The seventh day is holy to Yahweh, and one keeps it holy not by *doing* things for God or even for one's fellow human beings. One keeps it holy by doing nothing.

I think Hui-neng, the legendary sixth Zen patriarch, whose teaching constantly returned to learning how to do nothing, would understand Sabbath. I can almost see him, magically transported into a nineteenth-century Hasidic *shtetl* or into an ancient Jewish village on the seventh day, smiling appreciatively: these barbarians certainly had an inkling of the truth one day of the week at least. But what would disturb Hui-neng is that after sundown on the Sabbath, the Jews do begin again to live as though work and effort and time are real, as though action does make a difference and salvation has not yet come in its fullness. Maybe Hui-neng would swat a few behinds with his fan, or pull a few beards. But his efforts would be useless, because his reality and the reality of Moses are not the same. The difference is that Hui-neng views the world either as total transience or total stillness, and for him there is no real difference between the two. The Hebrew vision sees both acting and being, doing and nondoing, as equally real and equally important. By observing the rhythmic return of Sabbath, human beings reflect the divine reality itself.

Pre-Israelite versions of Sabbath did not extend the provisions for rest to domestic animals, or to strangers and sojourners temporarily resident in someone's house. They probably did not apply to women either. The Hebrew Sabbath ordinance, on the other hand, is universal. Everyone, including animals, slaves and guests, must stop work. There is no elitism. In the Orient, on the other hand, meditation is practiced mostly by a privileged, partially leisured class. The vast majority of Buddhists in the world do not meditate. They pray or chant on occasion. Meditation is left mostly to the monks. In fact, in most cultures, East and West, prayer and meditation are turned over to a special elite. But this approach presupposes a society where some people work while others meditate—not a very democratic form of spiritual discipline. Such elitism has also dogged the history of Western monasticism, which is Christianity's way of coping with the clash between the *via activa* and the *via contemplativa*. Some people worked while others prayed. For the Jews, however, there was no such spiritual elite. On the Sabbath *everyone* stopped and just sat.

Sabbath differs from meditation in another way. Not only is it universal, rather than elitist, it is also ethical. For Zen disciples, "just sitting" has no ethical significance whatever, at least not from a Western perspective in which distinguishing good, less good, and evil possibilities is important. In the Sabbath practice, on the other hand, the loftiest of all realities, God himself, is linked to the human needs of the lowest bonded servant. The link is a rare Hebrew verb ("to rest") found only twice in the entire Bible. It means, as we have seen, "to draw one's breath." Both Yahweh and the exhausted slave need to stop and catch their breath, to look up from the task at hand. As the sovereign of the universe, Yahweh can presumably pause whenever he chooses. But the kitchen slave and the grape picker must be protected by divine law from the greed and insensitivity of the rich. The Sabbath discipline is not just an option. It is a legal mandate in order to insure the extension of its full benefits to the poor and the powerless. One ancient version of the Sabbath rule underlines its seriousness by imposing the death penalty on anyone who works or who *makes someone else work* on Sabbath.

Few Jewish practices are more misunderstood by Christians than the Sabbath. One reason for this misunderstanding is that several of the stories of Jesus in the Gospels depict him as deliberately breaking Sabbath rules, especially by healing people. Because of the way these stories are often interpreted in sermons and church-school lessons, many Christians grow up with an image of the Jewish Sabbath as an unsparingly legalistic straitjacket or an empty attempt to observe meaningless ritual rules. No doubt there were abuses of the spirit of the Sabbath in Jesus' time. But most Christian educational material fails utterly to point out why the Sabbath was instituted or to describe its ingenious blending of contemplative and ethical purposes. Its importance has been further obscured where Jews have changed it from an ethical-universal discipline into a badge of ethnic and religious identity, and where zealous Christian "sabbatarians" have tried to enforce blue laws against Sunday sports entertainment and closing hours, conveying the impression that a Sabbath (now a Sunday) is perversely designed to prevent anyone from enjoying anything.

The spirit of Sabbath is a biblical equivalent of meditation. It nurtures the same kind of awareness that meditation nurtures, for Sabbath is not just a day for doing nothing. It is a particular form of consciousness, a way of thinking and being that strongly resembles what the Buddhists call "mindfulness." In the Hasidic tradition, where it reached its clearest expression, Sabbath not only excludes our ordinary forms of intervening and ordering, it also excludes manipulative ways of thinking about the world. Abraham Heschel repeats a story that exemplifies this point well. A certain rabbi, it seems, who was renowned for his wisdom and piety, and especially for his zeal in keeping Sabbath, once took a leisurely walk in his garden on the Sabbath day—an activity which even the severest interpreters allowed. Strolling in the shade of the branches the rabbi noticed that one of the apple trees badly needed pruning. Recognizing that, of course, such a thing could not be done on the seventh day, the rabbi nonetheless made a mental note to himself that he would see to the pruning early the next week. The Sabbath passed. But when the rabbi went out to the tree a few days later with ladder and clippers, he found it shriveled and lifeless. God had destroyed the apple tree to teach the rabbi that even *thinking* about work on the Sabbath is a violation of the commandment and of the true spirit of the Holy Day.

It is a matter of consciousness. When we plan to prune a tree, we perceive it differently than we do when we are simply aware of it, allowing it—for the moment at least—simply to be as it is. The Buddhist scriptures make this same point in a distinction they frequently draw between two forms of consciousness, which are often confused with each other. The first they call *sati,* usually translated with the English word "mindfulness." This is the "bare awareness" which is strengthened by the practice of meditation. It is being aware, fully aware of the apple tree, but having no judgments, plans or prospects for it. This *sati* is then often contrasted in the Buddhist texts with *sampajanna,* a form of consciousness which is sometimes translated as "clear comprehension." It refers to the attitude appropriate to doing something. *Sati* is receptive, open, passive. *Sampajanna* comes into play when action is required. According to the Buddhist notion, the two must be carefully distinguished and separately nourished before they can be correctly combined into what the texts call *satipatthana,* or "right mindfulness." Meditation is the cultivation of the first, receptive state of awareness, *sati.* Its purpose thus seems nearly identical with that of Sabbath.

Can we ever regain the glorious vision of Sabbath as a radiant queen, a jeweled sovereign who comes to visit bringing warmth and joy in her train? The poor and often inept Hasidic Jews in the stories of Isaac Bashevis Singer may bicker and complain, and they surely suffer, but when the sun goes down and the lamps begin to flicker on Friday evening, a kind of magic touches their world. Special cakes have been baked, and now the sacred candles are lighted. Sabbath is eternity in time, as Abraham Heschel says; it is a cathedral made not with stones and glass but with hours and minutes. It is a sacred symbol that no one can tear down or destroy. It comes every week, inviting human beings not to strive and succeed, not even to pray very much, but to taste and know that God is good, that the earth and the flesh are there to be shared and enjoyed.

To rediscover in our time this underlying human meaning of the Sabbath should make Jewish young people think twice about whether they want to follow in the footsteps of "enlightened" parents who have shied away from Sabbath observance as an embarrassment. And it should cause Christians to wonder how some of the seventh-day spell, so spoiled by misguided Puritan opposition to enjoying its freedom, can be found again.

It is foolish, however, to imagine that a general observance of Sabbath can be reinstituted in our time. Bringing back an old-fashioned Sabbath would require either a religiously unified culture—which we obviously do not have—or a tight and self-conscious subculture, which Jews once had but do not have any longer. We already have empty time, and major industries devoted to filling that time for us. Empty time is neither Sabbath nor meditation. What we need is a form of Sabbath observance which can be practiced in the modern, pluralistic world, which can function on an individual or a small group basis, but which restores the lost dialectic of action and repose, of intervention and letting be.

Meditation could become a modern equivalent of Sabbath. Sabbath is the key to a biblical understanding of meditation. True, meditation does not take the place of the gathered congregation, of celebrating and breaking bread. But it can restore the Sabbath insight that despite all the things that *must* be done in the world—to feed and liberate and heal—even God occasionally pauses to draw breath. Sabbath is a reminder that there will again be a time, as there once was a time, when toil and pain will cease, when play and song and just sitting will fill out the hours and days, when we will no longer require the rhythm of work and repose because there will be no real difference between them. Sabbath reminds us that that day will come, but it also reminds us that that day is not yet here. We need both reminders.

Our problem is that we need Sabbath but we live in a society whose pluralism militates against a particular day, shared by all, in which being replaces doing, and affirming takes precedence over accumulating. It seems unlikely that a common Sabbath can be recovered. For the time being we will have to get along on a somewhat more personal version of the Sabbath. The person whose vision of the world is derived from biblical faith rather than from the wisdom of the Orient can incorporate meditation as a part of a daily dialectic of withdrawal and involvement, of clarification and action. For inevitably, on this earth and in our history, we cannot live in an eternal Sabbath. We always have to go back again to those other six days, days which, though suffused with the memory and anticipation of Sabbath, are still days when action makes a difference.

The greed of an acquisitive society, the pace of industrial production—signaled by lights that never go out and belts that move day and night, all week and all year—the historic Christian contempt for the Jewish religious vision, the compulsive rationalism of a truncated form of science, all these have conspired to create a mindset in the modern West for which the wisdom of the East, the inevitable shadow of self, is bound to hold an immense appeal. But the Eastern path, as its wisest interpreters know full well, will never accommodate more than a few converts. Its ultimate answer, or non-answer, if it ever triumphed in the West, would do so at the cost of much that is valuable in the Western ethical and religious tradition. The wisest of the Zen masters will eventually inform us to look more closely at the land from which we have ridden off to seek enlightenment. If we do, we may discover that meditation can restore a lost treasure, the Fourth Commandment. It may be tarnished and twisted out of shape, but it still belongs to us; and as creatures who must live amid the contradictions and dislocations of history, the mini-Sabbath of meditation can be the gift of life itself.

I arrived back in Cambridge-Benares from the American Tibet not only having learned how to meditate, but also with the beginnings of a way to integrate my meditational practice into my own religious tradition. This had come about because a wise rabbi had not abandoned God's gift of Sabbath. I had learned what it means to be a Christian who practices a "Buddhist" form of meditation—from the Jews.

6 The Pool of Narcissus: The Psychologizing of Meditation

The descent from the moutain is never easy. My return from Naropa was made even more difficult by the fact that I had a hard time finding people to talk to about what had happened there. It was still summer, so most of my students were not around. Also, the people I most wanted to talk with seemed uninterested—and those who were willing to listen seemed to be interested for the wrong reasons. The fact is that the ministers and theologians I sought out were polite but evasive. The people who pressed me most avidly were mainly practicing psychologists and psychotherapists—or aspiring ones. Eastern spirituality seemed to bore the priests and fascinate the shrinks.

Part of the reason for this curious phenomenon is that some of the Eastern teachers have consciously chosen to present their ideas in Western psychological language. Trungpa himself, for example, often prefers to describe the human problem as "psychological pollution" and his goal as "sanity" (rather than "enlightenment"). Other gurus talk a lot about tranquility, inner peace and serenity. The other reason for the psychologist's fascination with the East, however, is that Western psychology itself is now floundering badly and many psychologists are eagerly turning to Eastern teaching as a possible means of deliverance.

One can understand why the psychotherapists are flocking to the gurus—some psychologists, like Baba Ram Dass, actually becoming gurus. Psychology, after all, is supposed to be the "science of the soul." But most Western psychologies, and the therapies that grow from them, premised as they are on the assumptions of modern science, find it burdensome to deal with "soul" at all. The reason for the difficulty is not hard to uncover. "Soul" and "psyche" are stubbornly religious words, and have been for most of their histories. But modern psychology tries to comprehend the psyche without reference to the vaster and more encompassing whole to which the teachings of all the great religions point. All psychologists today are in part children of the Enlightenment and of its condescending attitude toward superstition and spirituality. They are alienated by the history of their discipline from most of their own Western religious tradition. Consequently, when they begin to look for a new basis for the science of the soul, they usually turn toward the East.

It is not a new impulse. From the earliest decades of the nineteenth century, whenever Western intellectuals begin to feel disillusioned with the limits of science or the Enlightenment, they have almost always looked to the Orient for a fresh transfusion of magic or mysticism. Students of intellectual history have a name for this recurrent Western tendency. They call it "Orientalism." It should come as no surprise, therefore, to discover that Western psychology today is reenacting the same trope. The problem is that previous episodes of Orientalism have not restored the spiritual dimension to Western science but, on the contrary, have deepened the split between science and religion, thus rendering science more rigid and religion less self-critical. Western psychology's present love affair with the Orient seems to me just as unpromising and possibly even dangerous. The danger lies in the enormous power psychological ways of thinking now wield in our culture, a power so vast that the current psychologizing of Eastern contemplative disciplines—unless it is preceded by a thorough revolution in Western psychology itself—could rob these disciplines of their spiritual substance. It could pervert them into Western mental-health gimmicks and thereby prevent them from introducing the sharply alternative vision of life they are capable of bringing to us. In short, the merger of Western psychology and Eastern spirituality would resemble the marriage of an elephant and a flea. It would not be a merger but an absorption. It would not cure the soullessness of psychology but would distort the Oriental teachings into something they are not. The elephant today is just too big and too powerful—and too clumsy—for the flea. If the marriage is ever to occur, it can only be when the two parties approach each other more as equals than is possible —at least on Western intellectual soil—today.

Why are we in danger that Western psychology will spoil the meaning Eastern spirituality could have for us unless or until Western psychology undergoes its own reformation first? The reason is that Western psychology—despite occasional claims to the contrary—still continues to concentrate on the *self*. Its focus remains the ego, the id, the psyche, the secret-me-inside—with only peripheral interest directed toward the integral enmeshment of the self in its society, its cosmos and the other immense traceries within which it lives. Psychology has accepted too readily the specialized function modern science has assigned it. It has backed away from cosmology, metaphysics and theology —the rich matrix from which it first emerged—and has accepted a reduced and even trivialized role for itself. The result is that some psychologists, including a growing number of clinicians, are beginning to feel that they have reached a dead end. Their effort to understand the psyche without reference to the psyche's relationship to other realms of being has resulted in shallowness and aridity.

But there is something in every self that balks at this reduced status, a divine spark that senses more ample settings. Psychologists know this too. Consequently a revolt is under way in psychology—or rather, several revolts are going on at the same time. Psychotherapy is now under siege from within by a whole new set of psychological romantics. The followers of Freud and of various schools of behaviorism find themselves attacked by one or another of the celebrants of madness epitomized by R. D. Laing. But this battle has no winners. While one side eulogizes the benefits of reason and control and the other extols the beauty of insanity, both parties isolate the self from any larger spiritual cosmos. Sane or mad, the soul remains miniaturized. Even C. G. Jung and his interpreters, who want to call the gods, devils and angels back into the picture, usually do so by packing them all into an expanded self. Western psychology, like Narcissus, finds itself frozen at the edge of an eternal reflecting pond, staring into its own likeness.

Into this troubled situation come the new Oriental teachings such as sitting meditation. Not surprisingly, meditation has already been seized upon, both by psychologists and neo-Oriental teachers, as yet another device for delving into the bottomless recesses of the self. The Western proclivity for narcissism has been given a new baptism. It has been sanctified not only as a therapeutic technique but now also as a sacramental procedure, a means of grace. Self had already been made ultimate, and now the quest for the true self becomes the path to the Kingdom.

This congenital narcissism, pervading as it does a culture in which the search for the true self has taken on all the marks of a religious quest, makes it virtually certain that meditation—divorced from an ethical vision—will be grossly misunderstood and misused. Neither in Buddhism nor in Christianity is meditation a method for self-discovery or self-actualization. In the Orient it is a step toward escaping illusion and ego, and toward seeing the world of impermanence and suffering for what it is. In Christianity meditation is one pole in the dialectic of action and repose, being and doing. Both religions reject the idea of meditation merely as inquiry into the self: Buddhism because it sees selfhood as an artificial construct, and Christianity because it sees the self only in relation to other selves, to God, and to a world abounding in death-dealing and life-giving powers.

As it becomes psychologized, meditation loses its capacity to move us away from our narcissism. Instead, it turns into an excuse to keep Narcissus poised by the side of the reflecting pool, to persuade him that if he just keeps on staring he will eventually discover something. The danger posed by this impoverishment of spiritual discipline has already been noticed by some psychologists. James Hillman, who began as a follower of Jung but has attempted in his most recent work, *Revisioning Psychology*, to move on to a more independent stand, is one. Hillman bases his work on the premise that all human life inevitably includes a certain amount of pain, distress, confusion and depression. He understands this "pathos," however, not as something to be avoided, but as a potential source of growth and change. He fears, however, that appropriating Eastern spirituality will obscure the place of this "pathos," and that our preoccupation with finding a self freed from terror and uncertainty, impervious to the cackles of demons or the songs of sirens, will reduce the Eastern disciplines into caricatures of themselves. Hillman regrets that because of the way many of the Eastern techniques and philosophies are taught in the West, the necessary pain and hurt of human existence come to be seen as " . . . but part of the ten thousand illusions to be encountered on the path of life, a piece of appearance . . . or even a load of karma to which one pays duty . . . evidence of the lower, unactualized rungs of the ladder." Hillman fears Westernized versions of Eastern disciplines will encourage us to " . . . meditate, contemplate, exercise through and away from them," but will not teach us to see these hard moments as occasions for valuable insight.

Hillman does not want psychology to become an accomplice in this denial. He sees the hard experiences of life not merely as illusions to be risen above or sickness to be cured, but as the very moments when "the soul's divinity" expresses itself most clearly. But when Western definitions lay hold on them, Oriental approaches become forms of denial, tricking us into thinking that divinity is always found at the peaks of experience, not in the disappointments and never " . . . in the sludge of depression and anxiety, the depths to which actual life regularly returns."

Hillman is aware that what he is criticizing is not the Oriental path itself, but the way it is adapted by Westerners. "In the East the spirit is rooted in the thick yellow loam of richly pathologized imagery—" he writes—"demons, monsters, grotesque goddesses, tortures and obscenities. . . . But once uprooted and imported to the West it arrives debrided of its imaginal ground, dirt-free and smelling of sandalwood . . . Eastern doctrines as experienced through the archetypal structures of the Western psyche become a major and systematic denial of pathologizing." (Hillman, 1975) His disquietude about abuses of meditation and of other Oriental disciplines is based on his expansive vision of what the "soul" should include. He believes the soul should be an ample arena in which conflicting forces swirl and contend, and that therefore the present Western quest for freedom from depression and for instant serenity (reflected in the claims, for example, of Transcendental Meditation) excludes whole ranges of human experience. He detects behind the farfetched promises of some of the gurus an anodyzing of experience. He opts for more chaos and jaggedness in the realm of the psyche, a willingness to court dimensions of reality that many Western understandings of the self would gladly eliminate.

I believe Hillman is right, that meditation and the other Oriental disciplines should not be thought of as methods for eliminating psychic turmoil. But what about the widely discussed "quest for identity"? Can meditation be used to facilitate it? Again, I think the answer must be no. The "quest for identity" is the current code phrase for the search for self. It is still a symptom of narcissism, but because of its scientific-psychological ring, "identity quest" sounds more acceptable to people who might find engaging in a lifelong search for "self" futile or frivolous. But the result is the same, and just as neither Christian nor Buddhist forms of meditation can be used for purposes of self-discovery without doing violence to their intent, they should also not be twisted into tools for an identity quest. Although biblical thought and Buddhist philosophy oppose the notion of a quest for identity for different reasons, both would reject it as a valid goal.

The tension between biblical spirituality and the "quest for identity" arises in part from the fact that finding one's identity for most people today has to do in large measure with coming to terms with one's place in the life cycle. Erik Erikson's famous monograph, "Identity and the Life Cycle," is a good example of how closely these ideas are related in most psychological thought. In the biblical version, on the other hand, the life cycle is just not seen as a dependable source of clues to the question posed today as the "problem of identity."

On the surface, the idea of a universal life cycle through which all persons pass, and which can help individuals answer questions about the meaning of their own lives, is a very attractive one. After all, everyone has a life cycle. It begins with the adjustment infants must make to the physical reality of being born, having parents and perhaps siblings, of having to eat and sleep and defecate and be warmed and protected. The cycle goes on to speech, sexual maturation, mating, work, child-rearing, and eventually old age. In some way, the theory claims, all human beings pass through this cycle, touching most of its points, until they die.

So far, so good. Nor do problems arise when psychologists go on to claim that they can observe, in various cultures, normal or healthy ways of living within each stage of the cycle. The problems begin when the psychological *descriptions* subtly turn into moral *prescriptions*. Soon that unlucky individual who lingers too long at one stage or whose eccentric way of being adolescent or elderly differs markedly from the way most others do it may be regarded as retarded or neurotic. A quirky individualist may be seen as having an "identity crisis." And that can only be resolved by finding again the lost place in the life cycle.

All psychotherapies, of course, need some working definition of health, and such definitions are derived from the cultures within which the therapies function. Once a culture's norms for what constitutes healthy development are set, individuals who fail to mature in the culture's terms can be desperately unhappy. Therapists and educators are often expected to help get such people back on the track. The theological problem arises when, either consciously or not, therapists start to equate this getting on the track with salvation, or when they confuse the social function of ritual or meditation with their spiritual purposes. When this happens, therapists begin to think that the goal of religion is helping people discover their identities. For biblical faith, however, and for many other religious expressions as well, this functionalism misses the point. Biblical spirituality with its version of a God beyond the social order is not just an integrating force. It can be disruptive and subversive. The Jewish boy who solemnly lights the candles and recites the Hebrew cadences in the ritual of *bar mitzvah* is undoubtedly being helped, psychologists would say, to make personal sense out of adolescence. This is fine as far as it goes. What is lost in such a statement is that the boy, in some region of his being, should be dedicating himself to God; and seriously following the God of Israel can play havoc with social roles. It can bring suffering and unhappiness. It can even undermine expectations of appropriate "identity" in a given stage of the life cycle. Sarah, the dried-out octogenarian wife of Abraham, discovered this when she found herself expecting a child. So did downy David when he was told to take an adult warrior's role before he had had his first shave.

The Bible is not a useful source for life-cycle identity models. It is full of "dirty old men" and precocious kids. Noah slips into inebriation and illicit sex when he should be exhibiting composure and dignity. God's call comes to Moses too early and to Sarah too late, at least for normal expectations. Jesus is confounding the elders when he should be working through the trauma of voice change. The biblical God seems to be no respecter of the life cycles of men and women.

This is more than a random set of counter-examples. The underlying theological problem is that "identity" can become little more than a cluster of traits which the individual learns from the culture and internalizes, the end product of a tough series of negotiations between that surging little id, which detests any form of control, and the social roles a society's institutions prescribe for folks at that stage. "Identities" constitute a society's self-understanding. They are created and perpetuated by its privileged groups and reside in the heads of its people. But they reside there precariously. One of the reasons for the unexpected popularity of the movie *Harold and Maud* is that in depicting a love affair between a teen-age boy and an eighty-four-year-old woman, the movie lampoons the alleged regularity of life-cycle identities and appeals to the secret scorn many people feel toward them.

A theology based on the "quest for identity" is bound to be conservative. It lacks that element of the ridiculous, the unprecedented, the custom-shattering which comes from the transcendent realm. The "God" to whom faith points is not the protector of the social hierarchies but the One who sometimes breaks down and overturns them. For the prophets of Israel and their successors, from Jesus of Nazareth to Baal Shem Tov, finding one's identity within any society on earth may not be salvation at all, but bondage.

Underlying the difference between biblical faith and the quest for identity is a profound disparity between two basic views of what the "self" is. For the identity seeker, self appears as some sort of inner essence. It is a core which, though it can grow, never does more than actualize a potential which is already there. The essential self may be covered by layers of encrustation or coiled in compact possibility; nonetheless, it is *there*. It can be realized, laid bare, if one's search is persistent enough. It is the psychologized diminutive of the timeless uncreated soul of Neoplatonic philosophy. We may be unable to see it now, so the teaching goes, because of the weight of the flesh, the darkness of the material world, or the blindness of childhood repression. But that inner essence is there, we are assured: the real you, waiting to be pursued until its now-hidden light is sufficiently uncovered to allow its glow to illuminate the darkness.

It is important to understand that this modern psychological view of the self as something to be searched for, an essence to be uncovered or developed, not only runs against the grain of biblical spirituality; it also has nothing to do with the self-as-illusion idea taught by most Buddhist schools. Buddhist practitioners would be shocked to learn that meditation might be used in the pursuit of something as phantasmagoreal as the "self." When meditation is interpreted in a Buddhist light, it is seen as a way to help us escape the misleading notion that there is any self at all to be discovered.

The quest for identity is neither Buddhist nor biblical. It is the impoverished modern heir to a tradition going back to Plato and beyond, which sees the soul as part of the changeless stuff of the universe. It is impoverished, however, because the characteristics which were once attributed to the universe itself are now packed into the individual soul. Thus the self/soul may unfold and flower, but it only actualizes an original potential. Its development can be foreseen and facilitated. Nothing totally unanticipated or surprising ever occurs. This self/soul exhibits all of the qualities of a "surprise-free" phenomenon. It is the microscopic replication of a universe modern scientists would describe as "entropic," in which fruition within a form might be expected, but nothing unprecedented ever occurs.

For the individual person, the trouble with basing one's life on the quest for an essential self is that it results in a mode of living that might be called "concentric." The self, instead of enlarging and deepening its capacities, becomes more and more like itself. Gestures become posture. If the "real self" I am uncovering progressively becomes the determinant of my behavior, rigidity and sclerosis set in early. My actions become predictable and my perception of alternative modes of life narrows. I lose my vulnerability, my capacity to be shattered, or even to catch myself by surprise. I fall prey to the spiritual equivalent of "premature senility" (Rubert de Ventos, 1971).

There is, however, another way of looking at the world and the self. To oppose it to "concentric," let us call it "ec-centric," not in the sense of "peculiar," but following the more literal meaning of eccentric: centered outside of itself. This eccentric view of the self comes to us from the Hebrews, and informs those schools of theology and psychology which stress *novum*—unprecedented emergence and novelty. The opposite of the "surprise-free" universe, its world is characterized by singular, unanticipated events and unique persons. It sees sickness in the average, and health in the uncommon. It is the world touched by what Christian theology calls "grace."

In the biblical universe of grace and surprise, the human self is not a timeless essence. It is an open, physico-spiritual field that is both the product and the producer of real change. As St. John says, "It doth not yet appear what we shall be." For the "concentric" view, time is a circle in which all things, despite their appearance of originality, ultimately return to an entropic *status quo ante* (a pattern betrayed by the word "cycle" in "life cycle"). For the "eccentric," time is an arrow in uncertain flight, and the self is not an inner essence to be discovered and developed but an unfinished and unfinishable poem, a unique statement for which no archetypal pattern exists. In this biblical universe, concrete selves meet each other as combatants and companions, not as separated particles of One Cosmic Self. They are centers of being who grapple, love and hate. This irreducible otherness of the other defines the biblical view of the self. It also provides the only view of the self or psyche on which modern psychology can build a new and liberating science of the soul.

Although biblical spirituality and Buddhist philosophy agree in their common rejection of the idea of the "self" on which much of modern psychology and the popular search for identity are based, their agreement on this issue should not be allowed to obscure the important differences between them. If modern psychology needs to go through a revolution and to reincorporate its lost "theological" dimensions—as I believe it must—these differences between Eastern and Western views of the psyche are of critical significance. The truth is that the biblical understanding of the self as a center of decision and will, a free agent capable of choice, is the source of both our grandeur and our misery. When this personal self is located in a world of other selves and in a universe which is touched on by Another Self, then the richest possibilities of friendship and mutuality—as well as their awful opposites—emerge. It is a high-risk situation.

Oriental thinking, typified by classical Buddhist thinking, moves in a different direction. By eliminating the whole idea of selves, it frees human beings from the trauma of relationships, but at the same time it precludes the possibility of love, too. Thus Buddhism presents us with a totally unsentimental, fully unblinking way of living in a transient world where deep relationships with things and people lead only to pain and loss. It is appropriate that the word "detachment" should have come to occupy such a central place in Buddhist teaching. As people grow older and experience the sting of impermanence, the loss of friends and relatives, the ebbing of physical and mental powers, this venerable tradition commends itself more and more. The problem is, however, that in a culture like ours, already steeped in the philosophy of "You do your thing and I'll do mine," the lofty Buddhist idea of nonattachment can hardly escape distortion. Westerners will not be able to practice the Oriental posture of nonattachment until they move not just beyond attachments, but also beyond an "I" which does "my thing." Real nonattachment will become possible only when self slips away too. But this is something most Westerners either cannot or will not concede.

What is the alternative? We live in a period which, because of its continuing preoccupation with self-realization, has found any form of other-relatedness increasingly difficult. This difficulty contaminates not only love and friendship but also anger and other "negative" feelings toward others. The alternative to both the Oriental idea of selflessness and the modern psychological notion of concentric self-centeredness is the biblical view that there is a self which, though capable of fear and hatred of other selves, is also capable of concern and friendship. In fact, this biblical tradition teaches that without such high-risk involvements with other selves, the self shrivels into a brittle shard.

Love is the central theme in the biblical view of life. The opposite of love, however, is not hatred. It is possessiveness, the deep-set human drive to control and own the other. Biblical faith is not naive about this human inclination. It recognizes that possessiveness cannot be overcome by self-improvement programs. One quasi-religious movement, the Erhard Training Seminars (EST) already dishes up a combination of encounter-group techniques, behavior modification methods and Westernized Orientalism designed quite specifically to enable people—for a price—to learn how to calculate their own self-interest more efficiently and consistently. EST represents a particularly vivid example of what happens to Oriental insights when they are grafted onto a program of ego expansion and self-gratification. EST is a crossbreed of psychological and religious ideas and practices all brought to the service of self-realization and narcissism. Needless to say, the distortion of the Oriental insight is virtually complete, and the trouble lies in our modern readiness to use anything to help us cling to ego.

Jesus taught that the power to overcome our compulsion to control comes from a source outside ourselves. It originates in the marrow of the universe itself, in the heart of God, and reaches us through other imperfect human beings. This is what St. John meant by the now so banalized teaching that "God loves the world." The word "love," however emptied it may be, is crucial here because love can exist only in a world where there are genuinely different selves. When Jesus and the prophets teach that I should love my neighbor as myself, they do not mean to say that my neighbor *is* myself. Love is made both necessary and possible because my neighbor is not me.

Eastern philosophies stress compassion or detachment or unification. But the best-informed representatives of the Oriental traditions rightly refer to Christianity as the "religion of love." To say "God loves the world" is different from saying "God is the world," or God "is" and the world is not, or vice versa. In Christianity and Judaism, God and the world are equally real, but different. And the relationship between them is, or should be, one of love.

The psychological consequences of this world view are considerable, and few psychological systems, East or West, have fully grasped the implications of a universe held together by love between genuinely different entities. Eastern psychologies, in their manifold variety, serve mainly to present the picture of how life can be lived if what we think are differences are actually illusory. Since there is no real difference, love is redundant. Despite claims to the contrary, many Western philosophies arrive at the same point, though by a different route. They see "the other" not in its full otherness but as an occasion for one's own self-discovery or self-realization. Immanuel Kant, contrary to what one usually learns about him in philosophy courses, also failed to escape this trap. Kant set out to fashion an ethic based on an individual's obligation to fulfill his or her duty with regard to the other person. This other person was under no circumstances to be regarded as a "means." But even Kant's attempt finally failed. His "categorical imperative" to obey the inner call of duty ironically results in one's viewing the other not as a real other but as that entity to whom I am now fulfilling an obligation, thus contributing to my self-development as a duty-doing creature. Aristotle was at least honest in his defense of the exercise of reason as contributing to one's own self-realization. Modern writers, such as Norman Brown, who define human beings in terms of their capacity for erotic feeling do not succeed either. The other person is reduced to the occasion for *my* experience of ecstasy.

In short, despite centuries of effort, most, if not all, Western philosophies fall short of an ethic of love. They invariably make other people into valuable investments which will pay off eventually in the dividends of one's own self-realization. As one of my favorite teachers, the late Harvard philosopher John Wild, once said, after a lifetime of reading and teaching in the field of ethics, "In fact every influential ethic that has been formulated in our intellectual history is some version of self-realization." Wild began his career in the Harvard philosophy department while such great teachers as George Santayana and Josiah Royce were still present. He started out as an enthusiastic disciple and interpreter of Aristotle. But as he grew older he did not, as some teachers do, become more set in his ways. He changed his mind, finally discarding much of his Aristotelianism and becoming more convinced that the Christian concept of "sacrifice" made more sense than "development," "actualization," or "self-realization." (Wild, 1959)

The idea of sacrifice as it appears in many traditions, but especially as it is used in Christianity, presents a clear alternative to Narcissus. It is something different from either the non-self of Oriental philosophy or from the self-realization ethic of modern Western thought. Sacrifice does not mean withdrawing from the other or using the other, but giving oneself to the other. The use of the word "sacrifice" as the pivotal point of Christian ethics as opposed to "self-realization" ethics is obviously not a strategy designed to win converts today. Self-realization is our reigning philosophy, and many liberal Christians, especially those practicing various forms of counseling, interpret Christianity as one more form of self-realization. From such a perspective, meditation can easily be prescribed as yet another aid to the realization of the self.

The trouble is that Christianity is not a form of self-realization. Jesus was no Narcissus. The Gospel is premised on my turning *away* from a concern about my own self, what Luther called the heart's *incurvatus in se*, and *toward* the possibilities inherent in reorienting myself toward something outside. It is not concentric, but eccentric. Self-realization views the self as growing and developing within a fixed structure: growth brings to actuality what is already there in potentiality. The term "sacrifice," on the other hand, indicates that the new must come with a radical departure from the old: real change comes by a process so jarring and traumatic that it is like starting all over again ("Ye must be born anew"). Also, the person not only effects changes in the standard pattern; the pattern itself can be altered. Sacrifice has nothing to do with self-effacement or servility. It signifies a style of existence in which we let go not just of what is no longer serviceable, but of what could still be useful and good in order to claim the promise of the future.

I have said that all the dominant Western psychological theories turn out, on close examination, to be based on self-realization. But perhaps it is naive to expect any more. Like most creations of any given social system, psychological theories are meant to order and stabilize. They rarely try to incorporate into themselves the radical Christian notion that love for the genuinely different is the key to the whole evolutionary process. So a necessary tension always exists between Christianity and even the most carefully constructed psychological theory. If our current psychological language bears the unmistakable mark of being a product of a profit-oriented culture—as the use of terms such as "investment" in persons and psychic "dividends" indicates—that should not be surprising. There is even evidence that the search for identity is a useful activity for dominant groups to encourage. People engaged in an incessant identity quest will not have time to ask questions about cartels and juntas.

Love and sacrifice are two old and worn terms, but together they provide the only promising foundation I know for a new psychology, or for a new politics. Love means affirming what is genuinely and radically "not-me." It also entails sacrifice. In Christian theology, God affirms the human world in the most decisive manner imaginable—by putting himself within it, allowing himself to be touched by it, becoming vulnerable in its hands. This is the meaning of the incarnation of God in the man Jesus. But even before Christ's coming, so the Patristic Fathers speculated, God's reality itself contained the affirmation of otherness in its inner life. The doctrine of the Trinity, so quaint and comical to the modern mind, is the symbolic attempt of those early thinkers to say that in God himself, that is, at the core of cosmic reality, there is real difference and real love. The three-equals-one idea of the Trinity may sound bizarre to contemporary ears. But when one contrasts it to most Oriental views of reality, its significance becomes clear. For most Eastern thought, unity is real, but diversity and difference are lower, illusory or less real. They are eventually swallowed in what philosophers call an "ultimate monism." Not so for the Patristic

Christian philosophers. They wanted to describe a God who not only loved what was externally different, but also contained genuine love and real opposition within himself. If the Trinitarian doctrine, because it has been confused with some sort of numerical magic, succeeds mainly in obscuring this insight, we should remember that the Trinity has nothing to do with numbers. It has to do with the one and the many, with stability and change, and with the relationship between dynamic centers of freely deciding action.

The key term in Hebrew scripture for describing the relation of God to the world is *'ezer*, usually translated by the English term "helper." But the lackluster word "help" fails to describe the kind of action the holy *'ezrah* brings or the difference it makes. This *'ezrah* is not first aid or dishwashing assistance. It has nothing to do with crutches and braces. The holy one helps humankind by entering so thoroughly into the human situation that it is broken and transformed. God "helps" and the mountains melt, springs appear in the wilderness, and thrones topple. God helps human beings by liberating them from whatever prevents them from loving and receiving love.

Only when the revolutionary form of God's love is made clear can we then properly understand those well-known biblical passages which describe God as one who takes the form of a servant and who tells his people to become a servant nation. The purpose of this servanthood, as Isaiah puts it in chapter 42:1 is not to bow and scrape but "to bring forth justice to the nations." The servant or helper is not placed in a position of social subordination. Rather he or she brings to the relationship the power of love, which originates in the heart of the universe itself. These servant-helpers are ambassadors or agents, to use St. Paul's terms, of a cosmic energy that comes in weakness but eventually erodes all opposition.

In the decades to come Christianity will find itself engaged in spirited intellectual exchange with a number of differing psychological views of what constitutes the human self, the person, and the relation of a person to others and to the universe. All of these views will have important political and ethical implication. Some views, like the black-box behaviorism of B. F. Skinner, are so far from any religious definition of the self that the argument can proceed with some clarity. On two other fronts, however, the lines may become fuzzy, and both psychologists and theologians must make a continuous effort not to blur distinctions. From the many neo-Oriental movements we will hear more and more about "egolessness" and the "illusion of selfhood" and the value of nonattachment. In its classical Oriental expressions this philosophy merits attention and respect. But when it is watered down in such a way that Oriental detachment is simply added to Western ego, then we have the worst of all possible worlds: people using each other but avoiding entangling alliances. I expect this Westernized pseudo-Oriental pastiche to spread, and even at points to label itself religious or Christian. At the same time I think we can expect to see the growing use of meditation, and eventually of any religious discipline available—prayer, contemplation, fasting—to enhance the exploration and realization of the insatiable Western self. This will also no doubt be called "Christianity" even though it completely reverses the spirit of the prophets and Jesus.

I think both of these distortions of biblical faith should be unmasked, not to preserve pure doctrine but to enhance human options, to help at least a few people see that in addition to the way of pseudodetachment and the way of self-realization, there is also a third way—of sacrifice, love and risk.

7 Turning East

A few weeks after I returned from Naropa I went to my desk and pulled out the notes on neo-Oriental religious movements. The information was still there on the cards and scraps of paper, so I reread the interviews with devotees and the descriptions of satsangs. Although the handwriting was mine, the notes seemed to have been written by another person, an outsider. It was then that I began to consider chucking the whole idea of a book, not because I might be too critical of or too lenient with these movements, but because my own involvement with one of the disciplines had become sufficiently important to me that I did not want to bury it in a sea of descriptions. What if I wrote about myself with the same curiosity and tolerance with which I had written about other people: attentive but dispassionate, concerned but cool? It did not seem worth it.

As I read more notes and listened again to taped conversations, however, the temptation to abandon the book faded, and the clue I had previously sought in vain began to emerge in my mind. I had not become a convert. I had accepted and begun to practice a spiritual discipline for reasons of my own that sounded very different from the ideas of the individual who had taught me. I had felt like an East Turner *manqué*, a doubtful case, an exception. But as I listened again to the interviews, I heard many of the people I had talked to saying exactly the same thing. Each had turned East, in some measure or another, for reasons that each perceived to be unique to himself or herself. Although I had viewed them all as parts of a trend or movement, I did not see myself as simply part of a trend. And neither did they. All of a sudden I had found my focus. I would write about the Turn East as it looks from the viewpoint of an East Turner—not "the" East Turner, since they were all different, but from the various perspectives of various people who had turned that way. This would include myself. Now my criticisms would come not from outside, but from a critical "insider."

Who then are the "East Turners"? The people I am talking about here have not moved to India to live in an ashram. They have not left home to go to the Orient to dwell in a Tibetan temple or a Zen monastery, at least not permanently. They still live in Texas or Ohio or New York or somewhere else in the U.S.A. They have not *gone* East, they have *turned.* The term refers to those thousands of Americans who find themselves attracted today to groups, practices and ideas derived from one or another of the great traditions of Oriental spiritual wisdom. Their interest comes in widely varying degrees of seriousness and persistence. It extends from those who sneak a glance at a paperback edition of the *I Ching* or try some yoga postures to those who find as I did that one of the Eastern practices becomes important to them and to those who leave everything behind and sleep on mats in an American Hare Krishna temple. It includes serious seekers and frivolous dilettantes, converts and fellow travelers. But the fact is that large numbers of people are involved, not just a fringe group, and the extent of the interest has no precedent in American religious history.

How many are there? It is hard to say. The followers of the Maharaj Ji have sometimes claimed hundreds of thousands for his Divine Light Mission. The organization has two hundred local branches plus a string of food stores and filling stations. Although the spectacular failure of its well-publicized 1973 rally in the Houston Astrodome to attract as many people as expected casts some doubt on the figures supplied by the movement leaders themselves, and the public tiffs between the guru and his family have probably cost members as well as caused severe embarrassment, still, the movement has enlisted large numbers of devotees. The Tibetan Buddhists have attracted thousands of people, many of them artists, poets, psychotherapists and film makers, to Naropa and to their meditation-and-study centers in other parts of the country. Practitioners of TM (Transcendental Meditation) have organized meditation groups all over America and have started a university, the Maharishi University, in Goleta, near Los Angeles. The university's catalog runs to over 400 pages, listing hundreds of courses and institutes in a wide variety of subjects and featuring full-color photos of scores of faculty persons. Add to this the people who practice, regularly or sporadically, one or another form of Oriental meditation, or whose practice of karate goes beyond self-defense to its underlying Buddhist philosophy, and the numbers become significant. Although overall estimates vary widely, my own guess is that by now several million Americans have been touched in one way or another by some form of neo-Oriental thought or devotional practice.

Who are the people who are drawn to neo-Oriental movements? One way to answer this question would be to register the standard sociological data about the class, age, race, sex, regional residence, amount of education and ethnic background of the devotees of various groups. It is not difficult to answer this way, and such studies have been done. But this leaves much unsaid. We found that the participants tended to be young, in their late teens, twenties or early thirties. There are exceptions, of course. I met many people in their forties and fifties at Naropa. One of my most enthusiastic informants about the Hare Krishna movement was a fifty-five-year-old woman who had found some help among the devotees in dealing with her alcoholic husband. Although some early teen-agers learn how to do yoga or read a little Eastern philosophy, few become seriously involved until late adolescence. The twenties are the prime turning time.

In class and race, it is easy to see that the neo-Oriental movements are made up almost exclusively of white, educated, middle- and upper-middle-class young people. Most of the East Turners come from families that are comfortably fixed and have themselves at least begun to attend college—although some have dropped out after a year or two. Whether they intend to return to college largely depends on whether they belong to a group with a high degree of opposition to Western culture such as the Hare Krishnas or one that allows for or encourages compromise, such as the Divine Light Mission. Except for the Black Muslim organization, there are very few black young people in any of these movements, far fewer than the proportion of blacks in the population at large.

Women and men seem to participate in fairly equal numbers in all the movements, but men control the leadership posts. There is little evidence of the predominance of any particular regional background, although more devotees seem to come from urban than from rural areas—which is understandable, since one has at least to hear about the movement before one thinks of joining, and this is more likely in Chicago or Seattle than it is in a small town.

As a theologian I was interested in the religious backgrounds of the people we met. What kind of training or nurture, or lack of either, I wondered, would one discover among people who had made what appeared to be such a sharp break with their religious pasts? We did not always ask the people we talked with about their religious backgrounds, since this is often a delicate matter; and sometimes when we did ask they were not eager to talk about it. Some statistics are available, however. In his excellent study of the Hare Krishna Movement, J. Stillson Judah found that about 70 percent of the parents of the Krishna devotees he interviewed were members of a church or synagogue and that almost two-thirds of the devotees themselves had once attended their parents' churches regularly. Here are the affiliations of the parents of the devotees:

Roman Catholic	18.0%
Methodist	13.0%
Presbyterian	7.0%
Episcopalian	5.5%
Congregational	4.0%
Mormon	2.0%
Jewish	14.5%
Jehovah's Witnesses	3.5%
Other	7.0%
None	25.0%

Judah correctly observes that ". . . the large liberal Protestant churches whose church school attendance declined even more during the 1960s than their adult membership, contribute most to the membership of the Hare Krishna Movement." This is obviously true, but what strikes me in examining these backgrounds is the much higher proportion of devotees from a Jewish background (14.5 percent) than one might have expected in view of the fact that Jews constitute only about 3 percent of the American population. (Judah, 1974)

When all these statistics and categories have been reported, however, how much do we know about the actual human beings who have made this decisive choice? Not very much. This is why my students and I took another step in our effort to find out something about inner motivation from the East Turners themselves. Without using interview schedules, questionnaires or elaborate survey instruments, we simply went to the people themselves and asked them to tell us in their own words what they found in the groups they belonged to and why they continued to be a part of them. The answers they gave us varied in length, content and emotional tone, but as we sorted through them, despite the fact that every person had turned East for personal reasons, certain common patterns did emerge. There seemed to be roughly six clusters.

1. One thing people seem to be looking for in the neo-Oriental movements is simple human *friendship*. The reply we heard most, coming especially from people who actually resided in a religious commune or ashram, told a story of loneliness, isolation and the search for a supportive community. These accounts ran something like this:

> They seem to care for me here. I was bummed out, confused, just wandering around. When I first came here I didn't know what they were talking about. They all seemed crazy, and I told them so. But that didn't seem to bother them. They took me in. They made me feel at home. Now I feel like I'm a part of it, an important part too. I belong here. It's where I was meant to be.

We noticed that the shorter the time people had been involved in a given movement, the more often this reply came. After a few months or even a few weeks, however, the novices seem to begin to learn a more theologically "proper" answer such as "Krishna called me here" or "It was my karma." Many seekers who drift into such movements looking for intimacy quickly learn to express their reasons in the in-group argot. But clearly, the need for just plain friendship is the chief motivation for many of the East Turners. They are looking for warmth, affection and close ties of feeling. They don't find them at work, at school, in churches they attend or even at home. But they do seem to find all these and more, at least for a while, in the community of devotees.

This quest for a feeling-founded association is articulated most openly by the followers of the late Indian teacher Meher Baba. They like to call themselves "Baba Lovers," in part because the phrase itself contains a nice *double-entendre*. They love Baba, but they are also inspired by his teaching to *be* "lovers," that is, to welcome more affective and expressive relationships than are normally encouraged by outside society. Although few of the movements we studied made this warmth element as explicit as the Baba Lovers do, it was always there. Friendship is a scarce resource in modern society. The groups we visited provide an island of companionship in what the adherents feel is a world devoid of fraternity.

2. The East Turners are also looking for a way to experience life directly, without the intervention of ideas and concepts. Many told us they were looking for a kind of *immediacy* they had not been able to find elsewhere. I do not refer here to those who were looking for experience merely for its own sake, for another kick or another "trip" to add to their collection. That represents a pathological distortion of the quest, which I will discuss later. Here I refer to those persons who seemed to want a real personal encounter with God or the Holy, or simply with life, nature and other people. It also includes those who needed to find a kind of inner peace and had not found it anywhere else. Again, paraphrasing a large number of replies, the responses ran something like this:

All I got at any church I ever went to were sermons or homilies *about* God, *about* "the peace that passes understanding." Words, words, words. It was all up here [pointing to the head]. I never really *felt* it. It was all abstract, never direct, always somebody else's account of it. It was dull, boring, cold coffee. I'd sit or kneel or stand. I'd listen or read prayers. But it seemed lifeless. It was like reading the label instead of eating the contents. But here it happened to *me*. I experienced it myself. I don't have to take someone else's word for it because it happened to me. It's still happening. It was direct. I can never deny it.

This testimony of direct experience versus mediated teaching became more understandable when we noticed that almost all the neo-Oriental movements include instruction in some form of spiritual discipline. Leaders in the neo-Oriental movements show initiates the primary techniques of prayer, contemplation or meditation. Inquirers learn to breathe or dance or chant. They use archery or swordplay or acupuncture or massage. Teachers do not rely entirely on words but move inquirers quickly into the actual techniques—either quite simple, as in Transcendental Meditation, or very complex, as in Zen—for inducing the desired forms of consciousness. Unlike many of the currently available Western religious options, which stress beliefs or codes of ethics sometimes at the expense of a primary encounter of the person with reality, most of the neo-Oriental groups begin right away at the level of practice.

The most vivid example I found of this tendency to thrust the inquirer into practice, and to refuse to deal in ideas about it, came at the local Zen center. The teachers there not only sit you down immediately to face a blank wall, they also smilingly refuse to answer all but the most elementary questions until you have taken the practical step of trying to meditate. Even after that, they keep the ideas to a minimum. Practice and direct exposure are the keys to the kingdom, and if the responses of many of the people among the East Turners are to be trusted, this is one important facet of Zen's appeal.

3. Some East Turners are looking for *authority*. A third group of our respondents differed quite markedly from the second group. They told us, in one way or another, that they had turned East to find truth, to lay hold on a message or teaching they could believe and trust. They found themselves in these groups as refugees from uncertainty and doubt. Very often the people who gave this answer put a major emphasis on the role of the particular swami or guru whose wisdom or charismatic power had resulted in such a change in their lives. They gave answers like this:

> I tried everything. I read all the books, went to lectures, listened to different teachers. But all that happened was that I got all the more confused and baffled. I couldn't think straight anymore. I wandered around in a daze. I couldn't get myself together or make any decisions. Then I met [heard, saw, read] him [The name of the teacher varies, but the testimony is nearly identical] and what he said finally *made sense*. Everything finally clicked. I knew he was for real, that if anyone had the answer he certainly did. Besides, I could tell just from the way he spoke [the way he looked at me, etc.] that he knew what he was talking about. Now my confusion is over.

I call this reason for the Turn East the "quest for authority." It results from a wide range of factors that dozens of sociologists have documented: the dissolution of conventional moral codes, the erosion of traditional authorities, the emergence of what Alvin Toffler once called "overchoice." Although it could be cogently argued that we may have fewer real choices to make today (since the decision between Brand X and Brand Y is actually only an illusory choice), still the appearance of more choices is there, and it takes its toll. As a result, large numbers of people begin to suffer a kind of choice-fatigue. They hunger for an authority that will simplify, straighten out, assure—something or somebody that will make their choices fewer and less arduous. For some people the Teacher of Wisdom, touched by that mantle of light which the East seems to carry, brings an answer. The search for authority ends at the swami's feet.

4. A smaller number of people, though enough to notice, told us in one way or another that they had turned to the East because somehow it seemed more "*natural*." These people also appear to have changed their faith orientation more self-consciously than others and with deliberate rejection of what they believed was the effete, corrupt or outworn religious tradition of the West. They saw in Eastern spirituality a kind of unspoiled purity. In contrast to Western faith, to them the East seemed artless, simple and fresh. Significantly these people could often tell us why they had turned *from* some Western religion more clearly than they could say why they had turned *toward* the East. Although they said it in a number of ways, it came out something like this:

Western civilization is shot. It is nothing but technology and power and rationalization. A bloody record of war and pogroms and crusades. A monster: corrupted to its core by power and money. No contact with nature, feeling, spontaneity; and at its very heart is the Christian tradition which has probably made it worse. What we need to do now is learn from the Oriental peoples who have never been ruined by machines and science, who have kept close to their ancestors' simplicity, their inner feelings and the given rhythms of nature and the cosmos. Western religion has invalidated itself. Now only the East is possible.

The people who talked to us in this vein were often the most widely read and best educated of the East Turners. Many had read the Zen-and-nature poetry of Gary Snyder or the anti Christian polemics of Alan Watts. They could cite evidence more specifically and phrase their arguments more clearly than some of the others. Though they did not put it this way themselves, to me their choice to turn East often seemed to have some of the quality of a purification ritual. They were having a Western equivalent of a bath in the Ganges, shedding the tainted and the impure, choosing the pure and the innocent.

5. A relatively small number of people, mainly women, but some men, told us they had become involved in Eastern spirituality to get away from the seemingly total *male domination* of the Western faiths. They saw this oppressive patriarchy in both the doctrines and symbols of Western religious groups and in their patterns of leadership and practice. They looked to the East to find a better balance.

A male god creates a man who is supposedly led astray by a woman. There are male patriarchs and prophets, a male Christ and twelve male apostles. Male popes and bishops. Women are either virgins or witches or whores or grateful child-bearers. There is obviously no place in this religion for a woman. Now take the Hindus, they have Kali . . .

Significantly, the people who gave this answer were involved in one of the East-Turning groups mainly at an intellectual rather than a devotional level. Usually they were not very deeply involved at that. Though the inherited male-chauvinist structures of Christianity and Judaism obviously enrage many people, only a very few make it their reason for a serious turn to the East, for reasons that become obvious once one finds out that most other spiritual traditions have their own versions of male chauvinism, some of it even worse.

6. Finally, an interesting scattering of people told us they had turned to some version of an Eastern tradition as the result of a concern for health, ecology and the conservation of the planet's dwindling resources. Many of these East Turners also follow a macrobiotic or vegetarian diet or display a more than average amount of interest in the subtle but important relationship between the foods we eat and the condition of the spirit. Their argument runs something like this:

> Western religion has no real reverence for the sacred quality of the earth, the water, the trees. Since its God transcends nature and the Bible makes man have dominion over it, the result is that nature is misused and wasted and poisoned. Western faith is external and manipulative. Eastern spirituality sees the holy in nature and encourages a calm, noninterventionist attitude toward it. Unless we adopt the Eastern view and see that man has no more inherent rights than any other part of nature, we will destroy our planet.

The people who give this kind of answer may also hold up the American Indians or the Eskimos or some other group as having a more exemplary relationship to nature. But they usually claim that in one way or another the biblical view of human beings' relationship to nature contributed to the ecological crisis.

These then are the answers the East Turners themselves give most often when asked about the reasons for their turn. They are looking first of all for friendship and second for a directly felt experience of God and the world. In addition they seem to be seeking a way out of intellectual and moral confusion, a kind of innocence, or a way of life unmarred by sex stereotypes or technological overkill. When one examines this list of goals, it quickly becomes evident that the East Turners are not really very different from anyone else. They are looking for exactly what most people in America are looking for today. They have chosen a more visible and dramatic way of looking. The question, of course, is, Will they find it, there or anywhere else?

I believe that to respond to this question adequately, one must probe deeper than these actual replies to the underlying, often unconscious or unarticulated theological basis for the Turn East. When one does so, and notices that the Turn East is a part of a larger cultural malaise, the most ironic aspect of the whole thing is that it is occurring just as many millions of Asians are involved in an epochal "Turn West"—toward science and technology, Western political systems and occidental cultural forms. It is also clear in this otherwise confused situation, that East and West have much more than a merely geographical significance. Later on I will say more about the Western "myth of the Orient." Here it is mainly important to remember that, in the West, "Eastern" has always meant a certain cautious reserve about human initiative. For the Western mind the Eastern spiritual traditions have for centuries epitomized the archetypal image which Mircea Eliade identifies with "archaic man," while Christianity and Western culture have represented activism. Today, however, vast sections of Asia have moved out of the archaic pattern into a vigorous period of "making" their own history. And as they have, the religious traditions of those areas have become more activist, often drawing on strands that were there from their beginnings, unnoticed in the West, and sometimes borrowing insights from biblical faith. Just as this great awakening to history has begun to occur in the real Asia, millions of Americans have fallen in love with an Asia that is disappearing, or maybe never existed: the "mysterious Orient" of the old Western myth. Consequently it is misleading to see the East Turners opting for an outlook grounded in the contemporary Orient. The actual Asian outlook, as well as the Oriental faiths, is becoming more activist and more "historical," as Gandhi and Thich Nhat Hanh, a leader of the Vietnamese Buddhist antiwar movement, demonstrate. In fact, those who yearn for what they call an "Oriental" approach today are really opting for an "archaic" rather than for a "historical" way of life. They may be "turning back" instead of Turning East.

And they are in good company. The work of many of our most influential Western writers—T.S. Eliot and James Joyce, for example—is, as Mircea Eliade has written, "saturated in nostalgia for the myth of eternal repetition and in the last analysis, for the abolition of time." (Eliade, 1954) It is possible that in the current Turn East, what was once a hankering among artists and intellectuals has now reached the popular level. Below the surface of the quest for companionship and felt experience, and in addition to the other pressures that motivated them, it is possible that some of the East Turners of today are simply doubtful about the prospect of "making history," and prefer to sit it out. If this is true, and I believe it is, then it puts the challenge of the Turn East on a profound theological level. Why, given the calamitous history of this century, should we not be skeptical about the prospect of making history? Why not simply let things be? Surely the result could not be much worse than the result of centuries of Western history making.

Or could it? I believe the current wave of skepticism about the human prospect and about our capacity to influence history is mainly the result of the modern assumption that human beings are fully responsible for everything that happens, that there is no higher intelligence or grander purpose at work in cosmic evolution and human history. The Turn East is the logical outcome of the death of God. This represents a curious twist in intellectual history. It was once argued by secular humanists that positing the existence of a deity makes human beings lazy, that they will merely sit back and let God do it. The other side of that coin, however, is that when the tasks become enormous and the challenges nearly overwhelming, it is not the presence of a cosmic ally but the lack of one that drives people to despair.

This seems to be where many people who were once confident they could make a difference find themselves recently. The impact of biblical religion brought the idea of history and human responsibility for it into existence. But in its original version, this responsibility was to be exercised under the judgment and promise of God. In the modern and secular form of historical faith, God disappeared from the picture. Humankind was left with history to make but without cosmic support or any final source of accountability. Profit and power became the goals. The current feeling of powerlessness and the inability to do anything to avert famine or planetary pollution is the result. No wonder some people simply want to resign. In contrast to what Ivan Karamazov believed, without God now nothing seems possible.

The East Turners do not represent a way *out* of our Western spiritual crises. But they do help us understand it much better, in part because they embody it so clearly and often so attractively. In doing so they help us to understand and confront that part of ourselves which would like to abdicate history-making and let nature take its course. This temptation to dignified resignation has always been a part, though a repressed one, of the Western soul. It is especially evident now among many people —and I include myself in this group—who were passionately involved in the upheavals of the 1960s and whose hopes for genuine change were often disappointed. Eliade seemed to foresee the emergence of this mood of resignation when he wrote, just after World War II:

> It is not inadmissible to think of an epoch, and an epoch not too far distant, when humanity, to ensure its survival, will find itself reduced to desisting from any further "making" of history . . . [and] will confine itself to repeating prescribed archetypal gestures, and will strive to forget, as meaningless and dangerous, any spontaneous gesture which might entail "historical" consequences. It would even be interesting to compare the anhistorical solution of future societies with the paradisical or eschatological myths of the golden age of the beginning or the end of the world. (Eliade, 1949)

It may well be that Eliade's delphic prediction is now beginning to come true. For the "Western" spirit, inspired by biblical faith and now found in all parts of the world, not just the West, history is a challenge and a task. It is fraught with peril and promise, but it is an open process in which human beings have the responsibility and the freedom to make a new future. In our time, the burden of history and the enormity of the tasks we face have begun to make even the youngest and most energetic skeptical. Like the "archaic man" Eliade describes, we are tempted to step back from taking responsibility and to choose a world view that simply lets it all be. When I began to think about the various replies the East Turners gave to our questions—in the light both of Eliade's prediction and of my own experience—they began to make much more sense. What the East Turners told us were not prescriptions for a general cure. They were indications of a malaise with which we must all contend.

Take, for example, the replies that indicated a terrible hunger for fraternity and a search for a direct exposure to the real. These reasons for Turning East point to two tubercles in the body politic which debilitate both our churches and our culture—the erosion of human community and the evaporation of genuine experience. The first problem, the attenuation of bonds of friendship, has been discussed and deplored by sociologists and writers ever since the impact of the industrial revolution began to weaken traditional ties, and capitalism began to substitute relationships built on profit. Although the second illness, the substitution of abstraction for direct experience, has come to notice more recently, I believe it stems from the same sources. A way of life based on money, as ours is, ultimately undercuts both genuine community and real experience. It ingrains in us a way of perceiving both people and things as possible means to profitable ends. Even when we do not think about it consciously, our ability to befriend people is decimated, and our faculty for feeling deeply is corroded.

How are friendship and feeling made difficult in a society based on profits? Sometimes both the symptom and the sickness in any society can be illuminated by focusing on one phenomenon in that society in which they interact. In our society, prostitution as a business provides this focus. It is the most cogent paradigm of how both intimacy and feeling suffer when the market mentality takes over. There have always been prostitutes, at least as long as there has been someone to pay them. Ever since men have dominated women, which is probably since the beginning, there have been fertility priestesses, courtesans and concubines. The difference in our time is that cash payment relationships are not merely one type among others, they dominate nearly everything else, not just in prostitution but in education, art and politics too. Consequently sexuality, which is the place where intimacy and experience intersect, is bound to become distorted. In a sense, prostitution is an explicit example of what obtains in less explicit ways in all our relationships. We pay for what should be an exchange of gifts. We try to buy what ultimately cannot be bought. We use the money to purchase something—affection or experience —that can only be obtained by an investment of ourselves. The very possibility of human bonding disappears.

But the ability to feel deeply—about anything—also disappears in a market/money world. Since both people and things exist to be utilized for profit, one simply cannot get attached to them. The ability of prostitutes to avoid any emotional rapport with their clients is so accepted that the exceptions become famous. What is not noticed so often is that a cash-based culture teaches us to fear such rapport anywhere. But making oneself incapable of such involvements also systematically destroys one's capacity to experience anything else either. Anthropologists who have studied pre-literate religions rightly point out that capitalist countries display a kind of fetishism. They endow the symbols of things with more energy than the things themselves. Money itself is the principal fetish. Soon one does begin to "eat the label and disregard the goods." Not only is the capacity for experience gone, but the victim doesn't even know it. Christianity in a capitalist culture inevitably falls into fetishism and label-eating. Teachings *about* God and words *about* Christ and phrases *about* the Kingdom begin to replace the real thing. So the East Turners who recoil from the society around them in a desperate effort to find friendship and experience of the real have put their finger on something. They are right in their diagnosis. But are they right in their remedy?

Religious remedies for the ills of a culture take two basic forms. One is to try to get at the underlying causes of the malady. The other is to provide a way for people to live in spite of the illness, usually by providing them with an alternate mini-world, sufficiently removed from the big one outside so that its perils are kept away from the gate. The East Turners have almost all chosen the second form. The only solution they offer to other people is to join them in their mini-world. But if we all did, it would soon be a maxi-world with all the problems back again. Part of its answer is that it cannot be the answer for everyone. Some East Turners have found a haven from the impersonality and vacuousness of the larger society and, they would say, of its churches. They have rightly located two of the most severe symptoms of our ailing era, but their solution, though it may work for them individually, at least for a while, is ultimately no solution for the rest of us.

It would also be no solution, however, if we merely made our churches over into places where intimacy and direct experience are encouraged. This renovation is already going on in many churches and takes the form of everything from encounter-group liturgies, which purportedly facilitate intimacy, to pentecostal speaking in tongues which celebrates immediate experience. But the solution remains partial and stopgap unless the underlying cause, the organization of a whole civilization around greed, is changed. So the turn toward the East, like the candid mirror of prostitution, does point to a real deficiency in our way of life, not just an imaginary one.

Less cogent are two other reasons people gave us for their participation in neo-Oriental movements. Although the impulses they express seem legitimate enough, the pilgrims' hopes of finding any real succor in Oriental movements—at least for very long—appears remote. Included here are those people who yearn for a spirituality that balances masculine and feminine components better, or at least does not perpetuate male domination. I also include here the Zen macrobiotic dieters and religious vegetarians (as opposed to those whose non-meat-eating stems mainly from ethical and political grounds), those who seek a world view that endows nature with a more sacred significance than technical civilization does, and those who believe some form of Eastern spirituality can help us avoid an ecological collapse.

Although to these East Turners themselves such reasons seem compelling, I do not believe they raise questions that are as crucial as the search for experience and friendship. René Dubos, in his book *The God Within*, has already shattered the myth that only Christian cultures suffer from an ecological crisis by showing how pre-Christian Greeks and ancient Chinese also ruined environments. You don't have to be Christian to abuse nature. But Turning East for an ecological solution seems mistaken to me for a more obvious reason. The ecological mess we face is a macrostructural one. Unlike the other problems the East Turners are trying to solve, it is difficult to see how a merely personal way out is viable, even for a short time. The solution to this challenge must obviously be large-scale. The depletion of resources cannot be corrected by even the most stringent application of individual and small-group disciplines. While loneliness and feelinglessness are apparently solvable at this level, pollution simply is not. Even residents of macrobiotic communes must breathe the air and will die if the stratosphere is punctured (due to jet travel) or the polar ice cap melts (due to heat pollution). Again, if the only solution is for entire civilizations to convert to a new religion, for example Buddhism (which in any case has not prevented similar problems from emerging in Japan), that is no solution at all.

The people who Turn East to escape Western religious male chauvinism will also be disillusioned very quickly. They discover that patriarchy is not a Hebrew plot. If anything, the degree and scope of male domination in the neo-Oriental movements is even more pronounced than it is in most Christian denominations. My own belief is that both our abuse of nature and the perpetuation of male domination, however it started, is now integrally linked with the same profit-oriented mindset that deprives us of intimacy and real experience. Like the seekers previously discussed, those who look to the new Oriental movements to deliver us from our destruction of nature and the debasement of women serve us best by calling attention to a problem. But the way out they offer seems even less plausible than it did for the community-and-experience seekers.

Finally, in addition to replies from East Turners that are authentically challenging and others that are a little more ambiguous, there are also two kinds that are disturbing for another reason. These are the replies that reveal a quest that will lead not just to disillusionment but to frustration and bitterness. These include the replies that came to us from those people who turn to the East to try to regain a lost innocence—a world free of complications and shades-of-gray choices. One can sympathize with the yearning such seekers display. But one hopes people will eventually find out that since no such world will ever be found, religious maturity means learning to live in a complex, shades-of-gray world.

Also, the same qualms arise about the people whose talks with us showed that they longed deeply for an authority so unquestionable and total that they would not have to make hard decisions or chew through choices on their own. When it comes to quests for innocence and absolute answers, it is not the biblical faith or even its current expression that is deficient. It is the search itself that is ill-advised. In this regard the East Turners are right when they say they have not found what they are looking for in Christianity. There is no real Christian equivalent to the restored innocence promised, implicitly or explicitly, by some versions of Eastern piety. The spirituality of both the Old and the New Testaments teaches that men and women have indeed lost their innocence, and there is no immediate way to get it back—that in fact those who consider themselves most innocent are often the ones to watch out for most. "Beware of the children of light!" Often, at least for a while, converts to neo-Oriental movements do seem to find a kind of new innocence. They are "blissed out" and have a hassle-free life. The emphasis many of these movements place on the inner life, plus their relegation of secular society to an inferior form of reality, means that adhering to their teachings, even quite devotedly, will not create uncomfortable tensions at work or with the landlord. Since money and power and in some cases even the capacity to make choices are viewed as illusory or insignificant in some neo-Oriental movements, the causes of most political tussles disappear. The problem is that the nasty issues of work, politics and the rest do not *really* disappear. Eventually even East Turners have to grapple with them. But they must now do so with a world view that gives them little help, because it refuses to recognize that the problems even exist.

As regards the pursuit of an absolute religious and moral authority that will relieve human beings of the discomfort of making decisions, it is obvious that Christianity has all too often succumbed to the temptation of trying to provide it, as Dostoyevsky shows in his chapter on the Grand Inquisitor in *The Brothers Karamazov*. In that story the Inquisitor scolds Christ for expecting humans to become mature and insists the church must think and decide for them. But these lapses have been temporary detours. The central core of biblical faith points away from the infallible pope and the inerrant page. It requires a movement toward maturity among ordinary people, more personal choice and less dependency on higher-ups. This same direction can also be found in the cores of the great Oriental traditions, especially of Buddhism. But here we are not dealing with either the Bible or the Oriental traditions themselves. We are concerned with the way they have been used, or maybe even misused, to keep people immature. Nor does this entail any blaming of the particular individuals who in their pain and confusion reach out for some authority. People who hunger for this kind of authority over them suffer from the wounds dealt out by parents and schools and jobs where they have never been encouraged to flex their decision-making capacities. But in order to mature, the last thing they need is one more perfect master to solve their problems for them. They need friends and families and larger settings in which their confidence in their own capacities will be strengthened. Ultimately this, too, points toward the need for a whole society in which the making of decisions, instead of being concentrated in the hands of a few at the top, is diffused among those whose lives such decisions touch and shape.

After months of talking with those I have called the East Turners, and more months of reflecting on what I learned, I became increasingly grateful for what they taught me. Their often costly decisions to leave behind the values and beliefs of a system they found hollow moved me more than once. It reminded me again just how much people are willing to sacrifice for the nonmaterial needs of the spirit. Practically, the dozens of masters and gurus I talked with taught me some basic tools for psychic survival. I learned a meditation practice that I will always follow. But most importantly, they all showed me how urgent it is that Christianity break off its debilitating alliance with the spirit of profit, the demon which must be exorcised before it destroys us all.

I do not believe that the mere abolition of cash culture will solve all the hurts that pushed the people I talked with toward neo-Oriental paths. But neither do I believe we can take even a few steps toward eradicating the deepset evils that underlie the pain they are escaping as long as we retain a way of life explicitly constructed on accumulating and competing. Jesus might not have smashed the money-changers' tables if they had not taken over the temple. The market has a place in every society. It is when it becomes our faith, gold our fetish, and financial security our goal in life, that the confrontation must occur.

Jacob Needleman in his excellent book *The New Religions* concludes by suggesting that in the long run what the new Orientalism will do is to stimulate in the West a new appreciation for its own heritage. I agree with Needleman, except that he means mainly the mystical and esoteric heritage of the West; I mean something more. In the short run we can learn to appreciate those contemplative and communal aspects of our faith that have been hidden or denied or have atrophied through misuse. In the long run, however, we must see that a merely religious answer will not suffice. Only a profound change in the way we work and own and love will do that, and this will require Christianity to challenge deep-seated values and powerful interests. Unless that happens, the passionate quest for the human, so eloquently displayed by the East Turners, but felt by all of us, will surely fail.

One must begin somewhere, though, and here Needleman is right. My response to what the East Turners had taught me and to the questions raised by my experience at Naropa was to start looking for those ingredients of Christian tradition which my Protestant upbringing had hidden from me, but which I had long suspected were there. This began with a visit to a Benedictine monastery—Weston Priory in Vermont—and an unforgettable taste of the Christian contemplative tradition.

8 Buddhists and Benedictines: Christianity and the Turn East

The bell began ringing in my dream, a sweet unintrusive pealing, distant and melodious. But as the dream faded I knew the bell was sounding just outside my window, that Brother Richard in his plaid jacket and Levi's was pulling the cord, and that in ten minutes, at 4:30 A.M., the monks would be gathering for matins.

> O sing unto the Lord a new song:
> Sing unto the Lord, all the earth.
> Sing unto the Lord, bless his name;
> Show forth his salvation from day to day.

Without allowing myself the time to decide whether I wanted to get up or not, I rolled out of bed, sloshed cold water from the basin on my face, and pulled on my clothes. My visitor's cell in the Weston priory, following the explicit directions of St. Benedict's Rule itself, was scantily but adequately furnished with a cot, chair, table, lamp, closet, sink and crucifix. Little to distract. It was February in Vermont, and cold. I put on heavy socks and a wool sweater and picked my way downstairs to the simple common room where the earliest prayers of the day would be sung.

When I got to the room, most of the tiny monastery's sixteen monks were already there, sitting quietly on cushions in a semicircle near the huge picture window. Along the edge of the darkened hills across a valley, the gray light of the new day was just beginning to appear. Now one monk struck a chord on his guitar. Together they all sang, in perfect harmony, to a modern tune.

Calm is the night, O Lord
as we wait for you.
All the stars are laughing
at our wonder.

For a moment I felt utterly at home—with myself, with the monks and with the universe. For a millennium and a half, Benedictine monks have been greeting the morning with songs of praise. Here a steel-string guitar, Zen-type cushions and a melody reminiscent of Judy Collins had been added to an ancient ritual with no apparent incongruence. After the prayers and psalms we returned to our cells for a period of individual prayer, then gathered for a silent breakfast, then proceeded to the work of the day. Underfoot the snow squeaked in the 20-below temperature.

I was visiting a Benedictine monastery because, as is the case with many people, my encounter with Oriental spirituality had aroused my interest in part of my own tradition I had previously overlooked. Odd to have visited a Buddhist monastery before I ever visited a Christian one. But it was no accident that I had chosen this kind of Christian monastery. The Tibetans are, in some sense, the Benedictines of Buddhism. Although serious in their monastic life, the Tibetans have not shunned the world as many Theravada Buddhists and some Trappists and Carthusians have. Their monasteries performed in Tibet the same civilizing function the Benedictines performed in Barbarian Europe. Although both Tibetan (Vajrayana) Buddhists and Benedictines recognize that not everyone can or should be a monk, their communal discipline is a way to live together in the world, not a way to abandon it.

Among the reasons why people Turn East today, as our interviews and visits showed, is that they are looking for friendship, for experience, and for a teacher and a teaching that seem true. In Buddhist language, they are looking for a *sangha* (a group of serious colleagues), a guru (teacher) and a dharma (an authoritative teaching). The question that inevitably presented itself to my mind when I returned from Naropa was whether any or all of these might be found in Christianity itself. As I lived among the monks during those days in Vermont, I thought a lot about *sangha*, guru and dharma—and about their possible counterparts in my own tradition.

At first glance, parallels seem all too obvious. The search for *sangha* recalls the biblical idea of the covenant people, the congregation or the *ecclesia*. Dharma suggests a comparison with the Gospel. The place of Jesus, at first, seems similar to that of a guru. The question remains, however, whether or not there is real similarity below the surface.

1. Sangha and Friendship

Biblical faith recognizes the universal human need for friendship. In the Genesis narrative, God creates men and women to live in friendship and mutuality, not in isolation. But fear and possessiveness lead to betrayal, fratricide and exile. The Adam and Eve and the Cain and Abel in each of us destroy mutuality through jealousy and hunger for power: the result is loneliness and suspicion. But it does not end there. In the biblical saga, "God" is that nameless energy which pulls isolated people out of loneliness and oppression into a new form of human solidarity. God discloses himself primarily as the one who creates a nation out of scattered tribes, makes a covenant (*berith*) with them, and promises that eventually the covenant will include all the peoples of the earth.

The most significant feature of the new community that God initiates among the separated tribes is that it not only binds people to each other but binds them at the same time to God. The importance of this idea of covenant should not be lost sight of just because it is cast in mythological language. The inner meaning of "covenant" is that the most basic power of the universe is itself a source of, and a participant in, human friendship. Friendship is not something human beings must eke out of the wilderness themselves. Friendship includes the constellations and the oceans, and the source from which they all arise. *Berith* is no mere social contract. God enters into friendship with the world and with humanity. The covenant is not an incidental aspect of God. It expresses the divine essence. God *is* that which makes friendship possible in human life.

The concept of *berith* gives the idea of friendship a centrality in biblical faith which goes beyond even the notion of *sangha.* Since the inner mystery of the cosmos is both the originator of and a partner in the covenant, the divine presence within each person becomes the basis for friendship. This community is not based on mere consensus or shared aspiration. Nor is it hierarchical. Since all human rank and station shrink to insignificance before God, all members of the covenant are essentially equal. Leadership and authority are intended only to serve the community. Moreover, the basis of human participation in the community is affected by the nature of *berith.* People can accept and live in the community freely because they have not created it themselves. It is not some awkward arrangement which constantly needs to be mended or pumped up. In a community with such a grounding, people can let each other be. Since everyone in the community enjoys the same status, there is a quality of freedom that no mutual-interest society can have.

This all sounds good theologically, but it does not answer the question of why Westerners are looking for friendship in Oriental forms. What has happened to covenant community in the West? Like any expression of friendship, the reality of the covenant has been damaged by the acids of the modern industrial world. Eventually these corrosions will surely take their toll of neo-Oriental *sanghas* as well. But there were flaws in the way the covenant worked even before it was attacked by industrial values. In actual practice the covenant community, despite its cosmic grounding, never fully broke out of its ethnic definition. Although here and there in Jewish theology the idea of an inclusive human community is expressed, it is usually in visionary or utopian terms. In reality the covenant was mostly for Israelites.

The problem was not solved by the advent of Christianity. At first the Christian movement gave the covenant a universal quality, at least theoretically. In the great debate at the Council of Jerusalem it was decided that uncircumcised gentiles could also be full members of the *ecclesia,* the new community founded by Christ, and intended to appeal to everyone regardless of lineage. Christianity began as a movement of hundreds of tiny "societies of friends" spread around the shores of the

Mediterranean and tied to each other at first only through visiting teachers and the exchange of letters and gifts. But it soon became hierarchical and exclusive. Finally, when Emperor Constantine made the new faith the ideology of his empire and entire Visigoth tribes were baptized en masse, being a Christian meant joining an organization and adhering to a prescribed creed. The societies of friends soon virtually disappeared.

The early Benedictines made one response to this disappearance. It is often said that the monastic movement began in the West because thousands of individuals became disgusted with the church's subservience to the empire, and with the widespread corruption that accompanied its legal establishment. One may argue, however, that people abandoned imperial religion and lived in monastic settlements to reestablish a measure of communalism. They fled to the desert not to escape the despoiling of doctrine but to get away from the destruction of circles of friends and their replacement by a hierarchically ordered imperium. Christianity seems to have introduced the dream of a network of local communities united in a universal covenant—only to have lost it almost immediately.

But the idea of a covenant community was never entirely lost. Parallel to the official history of the church from Constantine on, there is another history of the restless search for a viable form of community where friendship could flourish. Bands of hermits, roving groups of monks, heretical movements and religious orders kept appearing. In almost every one of them the idea of spiritual friendship and sharing was central. It was the heart of the teaching of St. Benedict, who lived in the early sixth century. People took great risks and endured awful deprivation in these movements. During the five-hundred-year period from A.D. 1200 until A.D. 1700 in which the events we call the Reformation took place, thousands of efforts were made, most of them short-lived, to reconstitute the *ecclesia* on a more communal, less hierarchical basis. It would be tempting to reread the tempestuous history of Christianity not so much as strife over doctrines but as a series of attempts to establish an authentic community. The labels used by the various parties during the Reformation help to show what was at stake: "Papist," "Congregationalist," and "Presbyterian" refer to different theories of how a community is best organized, nurtured and governed. Christians, too, have spent a lot of energy in the search for *sangha*.

After 1600 the American wilderness received thousands of settlers who crossed the seas determined to found religious communities where fraternity and sorority would flourish. They often failed, but throughout the nineteenth century the United States was dotted with religious communes and spiritual utopias—in Ephrata, Oneida, New Harmony, the Shaker villages, to name only some of the better-known examples. I believe we can see in the current search for *sangha*, which has brought thousands of Americans to the doors of neo-Oriental groups, a continuing expression of a quest which began millennia ago and which has had an especially lively history in America.

2. Dharma and Gospel

With respect to dharma, or teaching, the East Turners, as I have already noted, are searching for a discipline that will enable them to meet both the sacred and the secular aspects of life with a directness not gutted by abstraction or sullied by analysis. Their quest represents the revolt of heart against head, which is also familiar to students of revivalism in Christianity. It is important to repeat, however, that for East Turners this quest for immediacy is not directed only at the experience of God. It is a search for an unaffected and honest encounter with all one meets—with nature, other people, and the self. Although some Eastern movements claim the techniques they teach can produce a direct relationship with the holy, others explicitly deny they can do any such thing. What such disciplines do make possible for many people is a way of coming into touch with persons and things without having to see them through a fuzzy screen of cerebral overlay.

Where does the screen come from? Here Christian and Oriental answers differ. I heard Ram Dass, the psychologist-turned-guru, articulate a typical Eastern answer to a large audience of enthusiastic listeners some months ago. Like many other neo-Oriental teachers, Ram Dass located the distorting screen in the phenomenon of language. He told of the problem he had eating pizza, an activity sure to bridge the gap to his youthful audience. Ram Dass said that in times past, just as he was about to bite into a large onion-mushroom-and-cheese pizza, he heard a voice within him say, "Eating pizza." The voice was not judgmental or mocking, just observing. Yet, putting the experience of eating pizza into words while it was happening detracted from the sheer taste of the pungent ingredients.

So far, I can agree completely with the diagnosis. All of us seem to have as a constant companion this loquacious little interior commentator, editorialist and observer. His running chatter constantly distracts us from the pure taste and smell and feel of whatever it is we are doing. Reality becomes increasingly hidden behind its labels. Chatter is distracting, which is why the Benedictines eat their meals in silence and the Trappists discourage any idle talk. How do we get beyond labels?

In Buddhist thought the word *dharmakaya* is sometimes used to designate the raw experience of being. It stands for the sheer "thatness" of reality, what is there before we name it or classify it. It is the pizza in the mouth at the moment when tongue and saliva and onions and hot tomato sauce seem indistinguishable from each other. *Dharmakaya* might also be described as the way of touching and seeing that the discipline of sitting meditation exemplifies. When one is simply watching one's own breath, no words or concepts are needed. But not all experiences are as pleasant as eating pizza, so meditation should not be presented as a technique to make life happier. Only a saccharinish form of meditation would produce exclusively enjoyable results. One who can taste pizza directly will inevitably go on to be able to taste anger, fear and pain more keenly also. That is why the experience of *dharmakaya* needs to be placed in a more inclusive vision of the world. It requires both a community of support, which in some forms of Buddhism is provided by the *sangha,* and an ethical framework, which Mahayana Buddhism supplies for many people in the ideal of *bodhisattva* (the notion that one does not accept the fullness of human liberation oneself until all sentient creatures share it).

In order to understand how the message of Jesus compares with the idea of *dharmakaya,* one must begin by noting that the Gospel is not a "message" in the usual sense at all. Jesus himself is the message. The Gospel is neither a dogma about him nor even a compilation of his own teachings. The reason the Jesus dharma centers in the life of a concrete historical person rather than in a body of verbal teachings derives from an insight which is not altogether unlike the notion of *dharmakaya.* The reason goes back to the ancient Hebrew recognition that no one can adequately represent either God or human beings in words or pictures. According to the Second Commandment, one should never use any image to depict either God or human beings or animals, and according to ancient Hebrew custom the name of God should never be uttered by human lips. All these proscriptions express the belief that since God is not just a transcendent being, but the essential constituent in the being of everything, there is something in every person and thing that resists labels. We err badly, this teaching insists, if we believe that what is real in the world around us can be grasped by words and concepts. We are commanded to make no images, not because it would be disrespectful, but because no image, no matter how carefully wrought, can possibly do justice to that which it is supposed to depict. All such constructs inevitably mislead and distort.

There are differences, however, between the Buddhist idea of *dharmakaya,* with its suspicion of words, and the biblical idea of the Holy, with its suspicion of trying to depict either God or human beings in any way. The difference is that where in most Buddhist schools of thought it is the words themselves that distort, in biblical faith it is not the words but our human inclination to use words to twist reality in our direction. Words themselves, and even pictures, are not, in the biblical view, essentially evil or misleading. But because we live as human persons in a world infected by possessiveness and hostility, we inevitably tend to use even the most valuable gifts in destructive ways. The problem is not language or concepts as such, but our misuse of them. Adam and Eve spoke with each other in the innocence of Eden. We lose our capacity for *dharmakaya* or direct experience (symbolized by the Garden of Eden) not because we use concepts and language, but because we try to control and dominate, seize and grasp. It is not the use of words that poisons our interaction with life; rather, our prior poisoning of life in turn poisons our words and concepts.

Since the Buddhist and biblical views of the locus of the infection differ, naturally their prescriptions for recovery vary too. Since in the biblical view our basic dislocation is a fractured relationship to the people and things around us, only the healing of these relationships will allow us to begin to use words to affirm people rather than to control them. The biblical faith teaches that this healing and restoring energy is available, and that as we are touched by it our thinking and speaking become less despoiling. For Buddhists, one slowly learns to realize that all the words and categories we use are illusory constructs, and this insight is itself liberating. In the Buddhist view we learn to use words sparingly because there is no way words can avoid distorting: "Words are liars." In the biblical view we allow ourselves to be weaned away from our need to grasp and clutch at those around us, and we find that this allows us to see and speak with less distortion—even to say, "I love you," not to control someone but because we mean it.

Both Buddhism and biblical faith recognize the validity of the human need for a direct encounter with the real stuff of life. Buddhism locates our alienation from reality in ignorance, wishful thinking, abstracting, concept-pandering. It has elaborated a sophisticated range of techniques and teachings for helping people to rise above this ignorance and face reality as it is. Biblical faith attributes our dilemma not to ignorance but to fear and lovelessness, our anxious need either to dominate the people around us or to keep them at a safe distance. Therefore the Buddhist path emphasizes overcoming ignorance, the biblical course concentrates on the restoration of mutuality.

Both the overlapping and the distinction between these two interpretations of a universal malady come to focus in the practice of meditation. Some Buddhists claim that the more they meditate the surer they become of the illusory quality of relationships. In my own experience of meditation quite the opposite occurs: I become increasingly aware that my life is constituted by relationships and that the health of those relationships is largely a matter of how much I am falling into controlling and allowing myself to be controlled by the people around me. When I return time and again to my departing breath, it is like taking a step away from the need to master or to be mastered, and a step toward the kind of mutuality which is possible when the liberating ingredients of any relationship are permitted to surface. When I get up from the cushion, my feeling toward other people is both more independent and more interdependent, closer and not as cloying, more integral and less entangling.

I agree with the Buddhist teaching that meditation helps people to respond to "what is really there." But included in what is really there is something that moves toward me from others, an energy that enables human beings to take a step beyond gamesmanship, toward meeting. This energy has its source not just in human beings themselves, but in something embedded in the structure of the cosmos. If I had to call it something I would use the word "grace." It is the mystery of grace which has the power to soften our hearts, still our fears, and restore us to each other. As this process begins, the poison level in our language goes down, concepts begin to function as bridges instead of walls, and one can accept people as God accepts them—not for what they can or cannot do for us but for what they are. A kind of *dharmakaya* occurs. Finally, we may be able to nibble a pizza without a troublesome little internal commentator whispering in our ear.

The Christian Gospel is a kind of dharma, a teaching. What it says, however, is that a direct encounter, a *dharmakaya*, not only with God but with our fellow earthlings, with nature and with our own deepest selves is in fact possible. The "message" comes, however, not as advice or exhortation. It comes in the only way it is credible, in a human person, Jesus, who actually did all these things and who points us toward other human beings as the indispensable clue to the discovery of the daily *dharmakaya* in our midst.

3. Jesus and the Guru

Jesus himself is the centerpiece of the Christian dharma. Was he then also a guru? Ever since he first appeared preaching and healing in the remote province of Galilee, people have tried to find the right word for Jesus, a credible way of grasping what he was about. In the pages of the New Testament alone, dozens of attempts to name and classify him appear. One group of followers, fired by a passion for the liberation of Judea from Rome, wanted him to be King of the Judeans, or the "Son of David," the one who would restore the storied empire of King David. Others wanted him to bring back religious purity to the Jews, to cleanse and purge and sanctify the nation. To these spiritual revivalists, Jesus seemed anointed by God in much the same way the great prophets and John the Baptist had been. Still others hoped this unlikely Galilean would actually become the legendary Son of Man mentioned widely in the popular piety of the day, a cosmic hero who would close the present world age with a crash and introduce a universal epoch of justice and peace, punishing the wicked and rewarding the righteous.

Jesus disappointed all of them. Occasionally he seemed to lend hope to the national-liberation enthusiasts. They must have been sparked with anticipation, for example, when he entered Jerusalem in a kind of caricature of the great Roman triumphal marches, riding a colt, with the crowds strewing branches before him. Still, he led no attack on the occupation forces and discouraged his followers from carrying weapons. Although he was finally executed in a manner clearly reserved for insurrectionaries, this happened because the local Judean leadership clique was obviously upset by his presence and succeeded in persuading the Romans that he was a menace.

But Jesus burst the hopes of the other groups, too. Those who looked for a great revival and a restoration of religious purity were enraged by his violation of ritual taboos. He would not engage in ceremonial hand washing, and he healed people on the Sabbath, which though condoned by other rabbis of his time, infuriated the stricter interpreters of seventh-day propriety. As if this were not enough, he completely dashed the hopes of the religious-revival party by associating with the ritually unclean—lepers and Gentiles—and by insisting that such pariahs would actually precede the righteous people into the Kingdom of God. He especially confused and disillusioned the people who wanted to apply to him the title Son of Man, which was the name attached to the coming hero of the popular folk religion of his day. He did this first by accepting the title, then allowing himself to be defeated, humiliated and killed, the exact opposite of the Son of Man scenario.

Jesus seemed determined to smash every expectation, label and title anyone tried to affix to him. He destroyed some by refusing the title in the first place. He destroyed others by accepting the title (Messiah, Son of Man, maybe even King of the Judeans) and then acting in a way that exploded what the title meant to those who used it.

Jesus would not be what anyone wanted him to be or do what they wanted him to do. Although he healed and taught and even fed people at times, he was not really a healer or teacher in the usual sense. When he cured people, it was to demonstrate the healing powers of the new epoch he claimed was dawning. When he taught, it was not to convey a tradition or pass on some kind of wisdom. Rather than teaching in the normal sense of the word, Jesus *announced* something. He pointed people to a spiritual reality he called the reign of God, which he insisted was now accessible to everyone and did not have to be awaited or anticipated in some near or remote future.

Jesus left behind him a trail of shattered illusions and wrecked expectations. When we say today that Jesus was in some way a key clue to the nature of God, this expectation-destroying quality of his life suggests what such a claim means. The God Jesus discloses will not be the God anyone wants. This God will not be a mere extension of human programs and aspirations. Divine "transcendence" therefore is not a matter of spatial distance or mystic fuzziness. It refers to the continuous power of the Holy to break through all concepts, doctrines, mental sets and cultural patterns. Jesus reveals God exactly because he was not what anybody expected or wanted. He refused to be classified, and he constantly forced people to deal directly with him rather than with their ideas about him. In doing so, Jesus exemplified in his life something Buddhist teachers constantly emphasize—that reality is always different from even our best ways of talking and thinking about it.

People's efforts to cast Jesus in a role that would serve their own purposes continued after his death. Even the pages of the New Testament are not entirely free of this redrawing of Jesus's portrait. Within a few years he was depicted as a dying and rising nature god in the style of Mithras. Later he became a frowning and all-powerful Byzantine emperor, the Pantocrator; still later a gentle teacher of virtue and charity, as the nineteenth-century liberals saw him. It is understandable that people over the centuries have tried to grasp the meaning of Jesus in categories familiar to them. Since Jesus cannot be entirely defined by any single role, this process will always go on. Each attempt has its own strengths and its own dangers. So today we find Jesus pictured as a circus clown, a national liberation rebel, a teacher of mystical wisdom, a preacher of feminism, an impulsive superstar or, as Kazantzakis portrays him, as a hot-blooded romantic hero. But because the spirit of Christ is still alive, the same refusal to be pigeonholed goes on today. No one of these costumes ever quite fits. Jesus still continues to shatter expectations and smear the pictures people paint of him.

Today, as the Turn East proceeds apace, there are two titles drawn from Eastern thought that some people are eager to press on Jesus. Both carry with them a considerable weight of Oriental metaphysics and theology, but once again, neither quite fits the one to whom they wish to attach it. One of these titles is "avatar." The other is "guru."

An avatar, the conception of which originated in Hindu spirituality, is one among many embodiments of the ultimate. Ideas of what an avatar is vary widely, but one current theory teaches that in each age there is an avatar on the earth somewhere—that Confucius, Moses, Jesus, the Buddha, St. Francis, Mohamet, Lao Tzu and many others were such embodiments of the divine. After these familiar names, the list of candidates begins to vary, depending on who makes the list, but the idea is clear: there is always a divine incarnation walking around on earth somewhere, and if we are tuned in properly we can locate him or her.

Although Jesus was probably not familiar with the avatar theory in this form, paradoxically he both abolished it and accepted it at the same time. He abolished the avatar idea, ironically, by accepting it so radically and so universally that it no longer made sense. He did this by allowing himself to be called Christ (or Messiah, which is the same word). In his time the title meant one who is anointed by God, a special representative of God among others—an idea not unlike that of avatar. However, Jesus went on to insist that henceforth God could be found not just in prophets, wise men or holy teachers but in all human beings. He emphasized the sweeping inclusiveness of "all" by especially singling out the poor, prisoners, sick and disreputable people, the ritually impure and the racially excluded as the ones in whom the presence of the Holy now dwelled. Jesus was the avatar to end all avatars. If we take his life message seriously, we need not rack our brains to figure out which of the current contenders is an avatar of the divine. All are, and none is; and the avatar we are seeking is already in the midst of us, in us and in those closest to us and farthest away.

If Jesus does not quite fit the classical role of avatar, then can he be understood as a guru? The term "guru" is also not one about which there is complete agreement. According to the informative section on the guru-disciple relationship in Herbert V. Guenther's and Chogyam Trungpa's *The Dawn of Tantra*:

> The term *guru* is an Indian word, which has now almost become part of the English language. Properly used, this term does not refer so much to a human person as to the object of a shift in attention which takes place from the human person who imparts the teaching to the teaching itself. The human person might more properly be called the *kalyanamitra* or spiritual friend . . . one who is able to impart spiritual guidance because he has been through the process himself. (Guenther and Trungpa, 1975)

The writers go on to say that although at a certain stage in the teaching process the guru may be identified with the *kalyanamitra*, this should not become a matter of personality cult. Eventually the teaching eclipses the teacher. Finally the world itself, as it unfolds from moment to moment, becomes the guru.

Can we see Jesus either as a guru or as a *kalyanamitra?* Soon after the death of Jesus a movement began among the first-century Greek-speaking followers of the new Christian movement which understood him as what scholars now call a *theios aner* (divine man). These early Hellenistic Christians saw Jesus as a superhuman figure, endowed with near-magical powers, the possessor of a kind of supernatural knowledge that " . . . he selectively reveals as divine revelation to those of his own choosing." (Weeden, 1971, p. 55) The majority of early Christians, however, rejected the divine man theology. It seems clear that one of the main purposes St. Mark had in mind when he wrote his account of the life of Jesus, the earliest Gospel we have, was to fight this first-century effort to make Jesus into the equivalent of a guru in our present popular sense.

According to St. Mark and the other synoptic Gospel writers, Jesus was decidedly not a teacher of divine wisdom who selectively imparted a secret teaching to a specially chosen few. He healed the sick and was reported to have worked other miracles. But nothing he did of this nature was calculated to dazzle audiences. On the contrary, rather than using his gifts to attract attention, Jesus often warned people not to make too much of the healings themselves. Above all, Jesus did not hand down clandestine lore. When he spoke, he addressed crowds in the open fields and in the synagogues. His whole life was devoted to warning people against teachings which were reserved for the select few or which required some rare gift of spiritual receptivity. He claimed that even the despised collectors of the Roman taxes could understand, and he seemed to go out of his way to consort with those he called the "poor in spirit," the religiously inept and the morally retarded. If we think of the title "guru" not in the elevated sense in which Trungpa and Guenther define it, but in its current popular usage as designating a superlatively holy person, perhaps capable of breathtaking feats, who secretly passes on some supreme wisdom to a selected coterie, then Jesus was no guru.

But can we understand Jesus as a guru in the more refined sense, or possibly as a *kalyanamitra,* an experienced spiritual friend? Certainly if the term "guru" entails a shift of attention from the person to the teaching, Jesus does not qualify. In what still appears to many people as patent arrogance, Jesus insisted that he himself exemplified his own teachings, that the two were inseparable. People eventually had to deal with *him,* not with what he said or with what was said about him.

Is this arrogance? I think not. It is simply Jesus' way of forcing us to deal directly with people rather than with ideas or conceptualizations. This is why Christianity has been correct in emphasizing that the Gospel points to a person, not to a system of thought or an ethical code. Jesus is a "spiritual friend" only insofar as he does what only a very close friend can do: he refuses to allow us to use him to reinforce our habitual patterns and our tendency to throw off the responsibility for our own lives onto other people. He did not permit himself to become the occasion for illusory hopes or passing the buck. He showed the anti-Roman guerrillas that if they believed God would cast off the Roman yoke they were deluding themselves. They would have to bring down the tyrant themselves. Jesus would not cater to the religious hopes of the people who yearned for a spiritual renaissance. He would not allow anyone to cope with him by using platitudes, conventional formulations or any existing *modus operandi*. Jesus was a unique person and as such he enables us to see the uniqueness of all persons.

Jesus is the person par excellence. In him we meet what we then realize is equally true for all persons: they are singular and unrepeatable centers of creativity and decision. They are not merely the occasions for perpetuating our own schemes or illustrations of our ideas or facilities for advancing our programs. Christian theology has correctly insisted that Jesus was both "true God and true man," not some well-blended admixture. He was fully divine and fully human. But in its one-sided reiteration of the "true God" part of this teaching, theology has frequently neglected to say that Jesus also shows us what a true human being is. This side is not only equally important; it is also integral to the "true God" part. No one knows what the "true God" side means unless he knows what the "true person" side means. Jesus is divine *because* he was fully human, and that which is most human in anyone is at the same time the *imago dei*, that which is most divine.

Jesus's final confrontation with the effort of his contemporaries to cast him in the role of guru or *kalyanamitra* came with his decision to allow himself to be identified with God—and then to be crucified. This was the ultimate overturning of dogmas and expectations. Whatever else gods do, they do not allow themselves to be cornered, railroaded, disgraced and lynched. Jesus had a clear choice. He could have refused the divine title, in which case his crucifixion would have offended no one. Rebels and rabble-rousers of his time frequently met such an end. Or Jesus could have accepted the title and then done what everyone expected God to do: destroy the oppressors, purify the nation, bring in an era of kindness and goodwill. Either of these courses would have made sense to his contemporaries.

Instead, Jesus chose a third course. He accepted the divine title *and* he allowed himself to be tracked down, tried and executed. The final destruction of everybody's fondest religious ideas occurred: God on a cross. In this denouement, Jesus put an end to any notion of God as the great guru in the skies, the magical *deus ex machina* or the omnipotent Big Brother. As Dietrich Bonhoeffer puts it in one of his most eloquent passages, "The only God who can help us is the one who cannot help."

After nearly two thousand years, the truth about Jesus has still hardly sunk in. Right after his death, stories began to circulate that he had escaped the gibbet, that a look-alike had been substituted, that while the crucifixion occurred he was standing on a nearby hill chuckling. Since then other people have tried to use the resurrection appearances of Jesus to reinstate the idea of a Big Daddy God who solves our problems for us and keeps us in eternal early adolescence. But the resurrection stories depict a crucified figure who still bears the wounds of the nails, and who gets hungry and must be fed. True, some current theologians object to this interpretation and argue that a crucified God cannot bring hope to the downtrodden and disenfranchised. Only an omnipotent God, they say, can buoy up the powerless. But Jesus knew better. To the landless peons of his day his life had an unmistakable message: God does not support the rich and the powerful, but neither does he intercede with magic arrows or well-aimed thunderbolts to remove an oppressor from the palace. God liberates the oppressed by enabling them to liberate themselves. This, I believe, is the only credible "liberation theology." Anything else feeds the kind of millennial fantasies which have kept the poor in bondage for centuries.

Was Jesus a guru? Is he a guru? The answer is that whatever

kind of guru one is looking for is the one Jesus refuses to be. He is an elusive figure, the saboteur of prefabrications, the true *kalyanamitra* who deftly places the ball back in our court. He is not the guru we want, but he is the guru whom, whether we know it or not, we need.

The monks at Weston Priory go to bed early. Since the day begins at 4:30 A.M. with Brother Richard pulling the bell cord, they need to. Also, the February nights in Vermont are dark and cold. Despite the arctic temperature, I took a walk the night before I left. The frosted air burned my nostrils and even the stars seemed to shiver. The monastery's dogs barked briefly as I crunched by, but then quickly crept back into their boxes. I felt cold, but comfortable. I was not a Benedictine or even a Catholic, but I felt that through the lens of these men's life together I had been able to catch a glimpse of something that was mine, something which in its own way could meet the need for *sangha,* dharma and guru that I had found not only in other people but in myself. I could see that, at least for me, Christian faith, despite the distortions which have marred it, can still answer the universal human yearning for friendship, authentic experience and even for trustworthy authority. But I also realized that it would be idle to urge the present East Turners to forgo their quest and return to their ancestral tradition. They have not found what they were looking for where it was supposed to be, and they have gone to look elsewhere. The only problem is that the same forces which have conspired to decimate the power of the biblical faith in the modern West will also inevitably work their spell on the Oriental traditions that reach our shores. The difficulty lies not so much with the traditions, Eastern or Western, as it does with the stony and unpromising soil on which the seed is scattered. To understand the chemistry of this stony soil, we will need to move on now to a spiritual assay of our own society in the closing decades of the twentieth century.

9 Enlightenment by Ticketron: American Society and the Turn East

On my desk lies a handsomely designed folder inviting me to an international conference on yoga and meditation. Sponsored by an organization in Glenview, Illinois, it is scheduled for the Palmer House in Chicago. When unfolded, the pamphlet displays the pictures and the credentials of no fewer than forty-eight swamis, gurus, psychological specialists on alternative states of consciousness, and practitioners of biofeedback and Oriental medicine. Featured prominently at the top of the first page, over the photograph of Swami Rama, who seems to be a central figure in the proceedings, stands the overall theme of the gathering: "Come Enlighten Yourself" . . . "Love all and exclude none—that is the way to enlightenment." The flyer indicates that in addition to thirty-five scheduled sessions, there will also be displays of art, sculpture and craft, " . . . each depicting in its own way, a message of yoga and meditation," exhibits of response-monitoring machinery, presentations of "the cultural and entertainment pastimes of East and West," and a widely varied selection of printed literature. A further note promises that "conference technicians will be capturing each seminar on film and tape" using either sound film or on stereophonic cassette tapes. The cost for the "total package" plan is seventy-five dollars, which does not, however, include lodging, meals or other costs. Tickets can also be obtained through Ticketron.

The business of America is business, and that includes the religion business. The greatest irony of the neo-Oriental religious movements is that in their effort to present an alternative to the Western way of life most have succeeded in adding only one more line of spiritual products to the American religious marketplace. They have become a part of the "consumer culture" they set out to call in question.

Maybe this accelerated consumerization of the new religious movements should not surprise us. After all, the genius of any consumer society is its capacity for changing anything, including its critics, into items for distribution and sale. Religious teachings and disciplines, Eastern or Western, can be transformed into commodities, assigned prices, packaged attractively and made available to prospective buyers. A popular mass-circulation magazine recently published an article entitled "A Consumer's Guide to Mysticism."

American history has recently entered a phase that might have surprised Thorstein Veblen, best known for his famous essay on conspicuous consumption. In our time, consumption of most things is expected to be *in*conspicuous. Except for a few hardy clotheshorses and jewelry displayers, the affluent of today are noted not for how elaborately they dress but for how casually. Patched and faded jeans actually sell for higher prices than those that look new. Big shiny new cars are bought only by well-intentioned but gauche social climbers who are still imitating Grandpa's climb to success. The children of the rich want outdated old cars with faded upholstery and failing mufflers. The unkempt young people who hitchhike across Europe generally come from families who could well afford the train, perhaps even the jet.

Conspicuous consumption is no longer a mark of distinction; what we have in its place is something I call the new gluttony. Gluttony is not a nice word. Many will confess without much shame to offenses of lust or pride. Few persons, however, would like to be described as gluttons. Yet I believe the idea of gluttony may help us understand our situation, including the flurry of interest in the Orient. Gluttony is the characteristic vice of consumer society, just as greed was the vice of early capitalist society. In classical theology, gluttony is one of the seven deadly sins, falling in most lists, significantly, just after envy and just before anger. Although the term has sometimes been reduced to mean overeating, gluttony actually refers to taking in or accumulating more than one needs or can use. In different historical periods the glutton directs his insatiable appetite to different objects. Today only the old-fashioned glutton still stuffs his mouth with too many entrees. Rather, he craves experiences—in quantity and variety, more and better, increasingly exotic; even spiritual experience is the object of the new gluttony.

The "poor little rich girl" in Shirley Temple movies sat at a gilded table in a palatial mansion, waited on by liveried retainers carrying silver goblets. She possessed everything a Depression population thought they wanted, and since they did not have what Shirley had, they were comforted to see that wealth did not make her happy. Shirley's counterpart now wears denim cut-offs and eats pizza, but she is accumulating experiences at a rate that would have dizzied the little heiress. Today's money is not chasing houses, cars and clothes, but travel, drugs, unusual sights and sounds, exotic tastes, therapies, and new emotional states. If disgrace haunts the new glutton, it is not for failing to *have* something but rather for failing to have *tried* something. Wardrobes and jewelry boxes may not bulge as much, but memory books are jammed. The very thought that out there somewhere lurks an experience one has not had now sends the affluent into more panic than their grandfathers felt when they discovered that another family in the club had commissioned a longer yacht. The affluent elite *look* outwardly very much like everyone else, but the chances are that they have been to more places and done more things and still look depressed, so the deprived viewers remain comforted.

The new gluttony transforms the entire range of human ideas and emotions into a well-stocked pantry. All that human beings have ever done or thought is stored there now, wrapped in foil and kept at the proper temperature, ready to be dished up when the experienced gourmet's appetite begins to lose its edge. Hermann Hesse may have foreseen something like the new gluttony when he described the "glass bead game" in his last and most mature novel, *Magister Ludi*. But in that story the residents of the fabled province of Castalia at least played imaginatively with the chits that represented all previous art, literature, religion and humanism. In our consumer-Castalia, the pieces are merely collected and devoured. The process is only cumulative. Nothing new emerges because it is of the essence of the glutton that he must hurry from one dish to the next lest he miss some fleeting taste or tantalizing flavor. He cannot really savor experience. He gobbles it up and goes on, letting the bones and pits pile up under the table.

No doubt economists as well as theologians could advance explanations for why we are moving from a greed-for-things to a gluttony-of-experience. In a system based on encouraging greed, people eventually become sated. It is hard to sell another radio to the family which already has one in every room, one in each car, and two portables for the beach. Of course, styles can be changed endlessly for common products, and they can be designed to wear out quickly and to be difficult to repair. Still, there is a limit to what most people can stack up.

With respect to experiences, however, there seems to be no such limit, and the experience merchants do not need to plan obsolescence or invent style changes. Their product self-destructs immediately, except for one's memory, and last year's model is unusable not for any reason so trivial as changing hemlines or fads in chrome trimming, but because it is gone. Economists can explain the new gluttony in the classical terms of a movement from goods to services. It is the old story of expanding markets, finding new resources and developing novel products. But now the product is an experience that can be sold and delivered to a customer. The resources are virtually infinite for the imaginative entrepreneur, and the market is that growing group of people whose hunger for accumulating mere things has begun to slow down.

Not all new gluttons were once old ones. They do not own piles of material possessions. But they have lived in a society surrounded by many old-fashioned acquirers. Having witnessed the futility of old-fashioned accumulating, they often lose interest in the race to acquire things before the starting gun goes off. But the gluttony remains. They simply choose a new set of goodies.

Theologians would not disagree with economists on the sources of the new gluttony, but they surely add another dimension to the discussion. Theology teaches that the most dangerous sins are those of the spirit, not those of the body. As persons and societies mature, their faults become more subtle and refined, less gross and obvious. Christianity teaches that the refined and subtle sins are the most dangerous, because they are the most destructive to oneself and to others. Jesus scorned the self-righteousness of the ministers and lawyers, but was so forgiving of those guilty of fleshly vices that he became the subject of whispers and complaints among the more conventional citizenry. Normally, as one's sins slide along the scale from flesh to spirit, one becomes increasingly subject to worse offenses, especially arrogance and self-righteousness. At the same time an even more lethal process sets in. All of one's venalities grow more ethereal. Lust moves from the loins to the heart. Anger poses as patience and martyred condescension. Even pride no longer delights in its own possessions but in its humility; and gluttony, as we have seen, does its own metamorphosis. If there is anything more unattractive than a self-righteous Pharisee boasting to God about his piety it is a self-righteously humble publican parading his lack of it.

It was the Spanish mystics who thought most deeply about the spiritualization of sin. St. John of the Cross warned his readers against what he called spiritual avarice, the focusing of covetousness and unseemly desire on the realm of the spirit. Here, also, he warned, there is danger in excess, and restraint should rule. One Carmelite novice master was in the habit of giving his charges only half a communion wafer at mass, to teach them to get along on less in the realm of the spirit as well as in earthly things. The consensus of the theological tradition seems to be that gluttony of the spirit is not only no improvement over its coarser cousin, but is even more dangerous to the soul.

Is there an element of spiritual gluttony in the current fascination with Oriental spirituality? I think there is. It must be quickly added that this is not to be laid at the feet of the Oriental traditions themselves, most of which are highly sensitive to the pitfalls of spiritual pride; awareness of this peril, for example, permeates the Zen tradition. Nor can we blame the often anguished people who are driven by forces they can neither control nor understand toward searching out more and more exhilarating "spiritual experiences." We have called gluttony a sin, and so it is. However, it is important to recall that in classical theology "sin" is not to be understood as a fault for which someone must be blamed. Sin is a bondage from which captives can be liberated. Jesus himself refused to be drawn into his disciples' bickering about who was to be faulted for this or that. He was principally interested in helping people to get disentangled from the grip of whatever was crippling or controlling them.

If there is any fault to be allocated, it lies not with the victims but with the buyer-seller nexus within which the new Oriental religious wave is marketed. Despite what may be good intentions all around, the consumer mentality can rot the fragile fruits of Eastern spirituality as soon as they are unpacked. The process is both ironic and pathetic. What begins in Benares at a protest against possessiveness ends up in Boston as still another possession. Dark Kali, the great and terrible destroyer, whose very glance can melt the flesh of the strongest warrior, whose slightest breath can stop the pulse and paralyze the soul, finds herself dangling from bracelets with all the other charms.

No deity however terrible, no devotion however deep, no ritual however splendid is exempt from the voracious process of trivialization. The smiling Buddha himself and the worldly-wise Krishna can be transformed by the new gluttony into collectors' trinkets. It was bad enough for King Midas that everything he touched turned to gold; the acquisition-accumulation pattern of the new gluttony does even more. Reversing the alchemist's course, it transforms rubies and emeralds into plastic, the sacred into the silly, the holy into the hokey.

The process of changing the gods into consumer software bears a certain similarity to the alchemy described by Karl Marx by which early capitalism transforms everything into what he called a "commodity." Persons and things subjected to this treatment cease to be looked at for what they are and begin to be viewed solely for their cash value. For Marx, there was something uncanny about this process. The commodity became a kind of astral body floating over the real thing, diverting our attention. Like the mad Pythagoreans of old, the stunned victims of consumer culture look at the heavens and instead of seeing stars, see price tags and numbers.

This process reaches its nadir, Marx wrote, when the human

being begins to see himself or herself as just another commodity devoid of genuine subjective experience. This disappearance of real things and persons cannot be corrected, he asserted, just by thinking about it. As long as the market defines value, and market value defines worth, we will all continue to wander like sleepwalkers through a nightmare world of insubstantial shadows, with even our own minds and bodies becoming the quotients of what someone somewhere will pay for them.

Whatever one may think now of Marx's predictions and prescriptions for escaping the ghostly world of commodities, there can be little doubt that his description of its strangeness still rings true. He saw that we live in a world where things and persons do not come to us with some inherent meaning but with a meaning infused into them by our particular culture. What Marx did not see is that the gods themselves are also subject to this awful metamorphosis. The gods of the Orient mean one thing there and something quite different here, and this is not to be blamed either on the gods themselves or on their original devotees or on their new seekers. It happens because when the gods migrate, or are transported, to a civilization where everything is to some extent a commodity, they become commodities too.

The cultural barrier which a commodity culture erects against the possibility of genuine interreligious exchange is thus a formidable one. It raises the question of whether we in the West can ever hear the voice of the East, can ever learn about the Buddhist or Hindu paths without corrupting them in the process. At its worst, the issue expresses itself in the paradoxical fact that although America today *seems* uncommonly receptive to spiritual ideas and practices from the East, the truth is that we are not really receptive to them at all. True, no stone walls have been erected to keep the pagans out. No Orders of Knights Templar have ridden forth to hurl back the infidels. The gates are open and the citizens seem ready to listen. No wonder many Eastern teachers view America as white unto harvest or a fertile ground in which to sow their seeds.

But curiously, it is precisely America's receptivity, its eagerness to hear, explore and experience, which creates the most difficult barrier to our actually learning from Eastern spirituality.

The very insatiable hunger for novelty, for intimacy, even for a kind of spirituality, which motivates so many Americans to turn toward the East also virtually guarantees that the turn will ultimately fail. It is the story of the Trojan horse, only this time in reverse. Oriental teachers need not sneak into America in disguise. Americans rush out to meet them, shower them with gifts, overwhelm them with attention. They are borne into the city as saviors. Only later do the teachers from afar discover that the precepts they have imparted have been heard and absorbed in such a way that the teacher would hardly recognize the results. Alfred Loisey once remarked that Jesus came preaching the Kingdom of God but what happened was the church. It could be said similarly of many of the current Eastern masters that they came teaching enlightenment but what happened was yet another spate of American self-improvement sects.

The problem with introducing Oriental spirituality into America today is that the cultural barrier which the light from the East must pass through functions as a thick prism. The prism consists of American consumer culture and psychological individualism. What emerges from the filtration process is something which has neither the impact of a genuine alternative vision nor the critical potential of biblical faith. Robbed by the prism of its color and sharpness, the now-refracted Oriental light serves as one more support for the structure its original teachers had most hoped it would undermine: the isolated, Western competitive ego. The effort to introduce Vajrayana (Tibetan) Buddhism into America, although it is only one example of the process of distortion, is a particularly vivid one and sheds some light on how the same thing happens to other traditions.

The two central tenets of this form of Buddhist teaching—something it shares with several other varieties of Buddhism—are the ideas of *detachment* and of *egolessness*. Few Buddhists would deny that "transience"—the fact that everything is always changing—is the main basis for suffering in the world, and that the Way of the Buddha is designed to overcome suffering. Therefore ego and attachment are the two main obstacles to tranquility and enlightenment. We suffer because we develop attachments, within and without, to something which by its very nature will inevitably disappoint and disillusion us. In fact,

Buddhists would say that the mistaken notion that we even have an ego, or that attachment is even possible, are the real sources of pain. The path of the Buddha is laid out for us, not, as is often supposed, to help us overcome ego and attachment. Rather it is there to help us to realize that, since everything within us and outside of us is always changing anyway, ego is illusory and attachment is impossible. We come to this awareness, however—so the teaching goes—not by understanding the ideas but by discovering this truth for ourselves in the process of meditation and spiritual discipline. Thus we eventually come to egolessness and detachment not as ideals to strive for but as accurate descriptions of a reality we had been refusing to recognize.

I find this central Buddhist teaching a challenging vision that, if taken at all seriously, would surely transform completely the way we Americans live and work and organize our society. I am not saying that I agree with this vision. It is not, in any case, a theory with which one can agree or disagree—and Buddhists generally refuse to enter into debates about it. Still, I think it can be maintained that egolessness and detachment lie close to the heart of the teaching. But prisms can turn blue into red, and it is dismaying to see how this truly alternative world view is so fragmented and recombined by the Western prism that what results is something far different from what went in, so different that it appears to be nearly its opposite.

The prism problem begins with the fact that contemporary Americans already experience a kind of "detachment," albeit very different from what the Buddhists have in mind. Our detachment comes from our living in a mobile, throwaway civilization in which we are schooled by the media not to get too attached to anything—or anybody—because we will soon have to discard it (or him or her) when an improved model appears. Our American form of detachment comes not from the spiritual insight that all things are moving toward nothingness, but from planned obsolescence, fashion changes and the constant introduction of new products to replace the ones we have. Our form of "detachment" is a kind of alienation that also infects relationships to persons, not just to things. It is the result of a Kleenex, paper-plate and styrofoam-cup way of life—itself the result of our economy's unending need to sell new products. The outcome of all this is that many Americans, especially from the most affluent groups, already suffer an amorphous sense of "detachment," an inability to form lasting and significant relationships with either persons or things. The rising divorce rate and the insoluble problem of where to pile our mountainous rubbish both give witness to our inability to care deeply about what is already there.

It must be said at once that this alienated form of consumer detachment is not what the Buddhists teach. They would see it as a pathological form of attachment; not detachment at all but a kind of insatiable grasping after something that cannot be grasped. Consumer "detachment" is not a part of Buddhist teaching. But it is a part of the Western prism through which that teaching must pass, and therein lies the difficulty. Many of the earnest seekers and serious practitioners I met at Naropa turned out to be very "detached" people whose lives had made them wary of the pain that can result from forming deep attachments to others. Many were divorced, single and adrift, or unhappily married. Many had moved in and out of careers or colleges, none of which had been particularly satisfying to them. Several had dabbled in other spiritual movements or in drugs or politics. They all seemed open, likable and friendly. But somehow I got the impression that they had no real turf, little sense of home or hearth, no person or purpose to which they were willing to bind themselves very deeply or for very long. Even those who were most wrapped up with Chogyam Trungpa, the founder and resident master of Naropa, seemed to appreciate the fact that he discouraged enthusiastic attachment either to himself or to his movement. They were people who had come to terms with the built-in transience of consumer society and who had found in Buddhism a philosophy that allowed them to live without guilt and without too many regrets.

Up to this point the prism effect, the distortion of Oriental teaching by occidental expectation, had probably not corrupted the core idea of "detachment" too badly. Although the two forms of detachment, Buddhist and American, are very different, even the distorted idea gave these people a certain amount of inner peace and personal support. The real problem enters, however, with the idea of egolessness and its prismatic distortion in the West.

There is no basis whatever in our Western experience for understanding what the Buddhists mean by egolessness. Here even the most eloquent Oriental teachers come to a dead end. I have heard learned and articulate Buddhists try every device they know to get the idea of egolessness across to receptive, attentive Western audiences—never with any success. Westerners listen, ponder, puzzle and listen again, but almost never understand. Worse still, they sometimes believe they have grasped what the Buddhists mean when they say "ego is illusion," when the truth is they have not grasped it at all. Except for the very rare mystic, or the person who has lived through a period of psychotic personality disintegration to which he probably does not wish to return, there is hardly anything in ordinary Western experiences (even, I think, after long periods of meditation) that even remotely connects with the key Oriental idea of egolessness. Here the prism becomes opaque. Not even a faint glimmer of light gets through.

The result of the failure of even serious Western seekers to catch on to the Buddhist idea of "ego is illusion" is that this part of the teaching remains a more or less dead letter. Though Western practitioners may talk about it, using the correct Buddhist language, one inevitably gains the impression that they are not really describing their own experience but are repeating a credo. At another level, beginners on the Buddhist path, stumped by the idea of egolessness, end up identifying it with something like the opposite of egoism, or with not being "egotistical." To them it sounds like the familiar moral injunctions against selfishness they have heard since childhood. Few realize the utter radicalness and frightening profundity of egolessness in its naked reality. This teaching just does not make it through the prism.

The end result of the Western prismatic refraction of the light from the East is a wholly new pattern. This new pattern combines the Western ego—only slightly curbed by warnings against selfishness—with an idea of detachment already distorted by consumer living. The product is in some ways a combination of the worst elements of both cultures. Western religion tends to accept the ego but teaches that love as a positive form of attachment can replace possessiveness and manipulation. Eastern spirituality does not give love such a central place, but teaches that ego is unreal, and that all forms of attachment lead to suffering. The prism-distorted Western version of Buddhism combines loveless ego with psychological "detachment." What comes out looks much like irresponsibility with a spiritual cover, a metaphysical license to avoid risky, demanding relationships, a mystical permit to skip from one person, bed, cause or program to another without ever taking the plunge.

Does this mean that the spiritual wisdom of the Orient, the light from the East, is fated always to be deflected—that it can never reach us except in a grossly distorted form? At first the outlook appears grim. Obviously, merely increasing the intensity of the light will accomplish nothing. A stronger light from the East passing through the same prism will only produce an even more grotesque monstrosity. Can anything be done?

I have occasionally met individuals who know how integral religion and culture are, and who have made a serious effort to avoid the prism by becoming deeply involved in a wholly different culture. Some have spent years in Japanese monasteries or Indian temples, adapting themselves to new clothes and diet and language as well as to unfamiliar techniques of prayer and meditation. Without fail, each of these bold spirits told me that as the months and years went on they became aware of what a nearly impossible task they had set for themselves. One man said that after his first two years in a Zen monastery in Kyoto he believed he was making real progress, but that at the end of five years he felt further from his goal than he had felt on the first day he shaved his head and sat down cross-legged with his face to the paper-and-bamboo wall. When I compare such patient and ruthlessly honest pilgrims with the enthusiastic converts who tell me that everything changed on that wonderful day when they memorized their mantra or opened their third eye, I cannot help wondering, in the latter cases, how deep a change has actually taken place. Is there any hope then that the new Orientalism can ever help us escape our captivity to commodities?

I believe there is a basis for hope and that the Turn East can eventually help us. Although it is easy to single out a spiritual cafeteria held at a luxury hotel in Chicago and to show, as I have done, how far it has abandoned the spirit of the Vedas or the wisdom of the ancient masters, there is another side. Any movement, religious or otherwise, which wants to reach people in America will eventually have to confront in one way or another the business culture. So far, however, the neo-Oriental movements have done so only at the individual level, and this is not enough. I do not condemn the eager spiritual seekers who flock to such conferences. They did not invent spiritual gluttony, nor did they create the acquisitive system which transforms their most idealistic quest into a need which can be located in a market survey and transformed into a sales possibility. They are as much victims as malefactors.

What is the proper response of the churches and synagogues of America to the new influx of consumerized neo-Oriental spirituality? Surely it is not the panicky utilization of the so-called "deprogramming" methods popularized by Ted Patrick's sensational book *Let Our Children Go*. When used on minors who have been kidnapped with parental approval, these techniques are nothing more than a debasing form of behavior modification that should be rejected out of hand by any religiously sensitive person. When used on adults, deprogramming is also plainly illegal and unconstitutional. It is frightening to me to see people who are otherwise alert guardians of the First Amendment's guarantee of freedom of religious expression condoning the deprogrammers when we are all aware that such methods could also be used—and have been used—on Catholics, members of Christian sects and followers of other religious movements. Some psychiatrists have even been known to lend support to the incarceration of the devotees of the Krishna Consciousness movement, for example, because they think that anyone who chooses a life of prayer and worship instead of a career must obviously be mentally disturbed. One wonders what these zealous defenders of psychological orthodoxy would have done with Jesus—whose parents considered him demented—or with Saint Francis or the Baal Shem Tov.

The most famous incident of deprogramming in religious history involves St. Thomas Aquinas, whose parents tried every device they knew to get him to renounce his religious vows. It is also pertinent to observe that the most assiduous efforts of the deprogrammers are directed not to the customers of Ticketron enlightenment but to those who, like the Hare Krishna devotees, exhibit a life style which is at radical variance with a society caught up in success and self-expression. I believe the religious institutions of the West should not rely on psychological deprogrammers to meet the challenge of the East but should do what they can, first to insure the freedom of all religious groups, second to expose the sources of the consumerization that affects all religions, including our own, and third to respond to the challenge at a genuinely theological level.

A proper theological response to the consumerization of Oriental spirituality should be directed not at its victims but at the underlying system which makes such a trivialization all but inevitable. In recent years Christianity has either ignored the sin of acquisitiveness or has also directed its criticism mainly against individuals. But this has not always been the case. At times, though not frequently, Christianity has transcended mere individualism and has brought the weight of its moral vision to bear against the gross injustice and dehumanizing effects of corporate systems. In the history of American Christianity, for example, Walter Rauschenbusch, the Niebuhrs, Washington Gladden and many others have reminded us that the acquisitive society is an enemy of the soul and that we cannot ultimately serve both God and profit. We need to hear this message again today.

The irony of the Turn East is that in seeking to oppose the system, it seems to reinforce it; in fleeing it, it extends its perimeters. Its tragic failure to make any significant impact at the inner core of our culture could, however, have at least one positive effect. It could help us to become more aware of our own shortcomings. It could make us see more clearly how badly Christianity has also failed in this respect. If this realization then stimulated a rebirth of the biblical social vision during a period when it seems to have fallen on hard times, then the Turn East may have contributed to our healing after all.

The American philosopher Jacob Needleman has eloquently addressed himself in some of his recent books to the issue of whether Americans can ever hear the message of the East. Needleman is concerned about the fact that sacred teachings, especially those emanating from the East, were originally transmitted only to persons who were seriously committed to the demanding disciplines of a *path.* The master conveyed the teaching to the disciple only when he was sure the disciple had made himself ready. Now, Needleman fears, these "esoteric" ideas (esoteric only in the sense that they are communicated in the closed context of a shared trust) have been made "exoteric." They have been placed on the market. Needleman puts it very strongly. We must understand, he says, " . . . the deviation that takes place when the formulations of esoteric ideas are 'stolen' from the personal disciplines of the *path* to be organized and promoted by individuals who are themselves in the condition of unconscious psychological fragmentation." (Needleman, 1975, p. 163) Under such conditions, Needleman fears, even the subtlest and most profound teachings are fated to become mere concepts, to contribute willy-nilly to the further reinforcement of ego. He does not seem at all hopeful that we can escape this awful impasse, since the "guardians" who once stood at the gates preventing easy access to the treasures now seem to have vanished. (Needleman, 1975, p. 170)

Although I share something of Needleman's grave outlook, I am not quite as pessimistic as he seems to be. Obviously, as he shows, spiritual ideas coming in from the Orient have begun to serve purposes that are often nearly the opposite of their original ones. For Needleman, the problem lies in the split between idea and experience, between personal discipline and truth, and the result is that teachings that were meant to undermine the whole idea of ego end up being part of ego's armament. Although I agree in part with Needleman's diagnosis, I see this split not just as an individual shortcoming but as the product of a centuries-long social development in the West—a development which is both economic and cultural—which has created in our time a characteristic personality: the competitive consumer of ideas, the compulsive devourer of experiences. When Needleman describes current Western man as one who "steals" the esoteric ideas to bolster his conceptual schemas, this is what he may have in mind.

The reason why I still hope, where Needleman seems almost to despair, is that I can never give up the conviction that change, even profound change, in a person or in a society, is possible. In its most original formulation, Christianity not only *requires* "repentance" in order to participate in the Kingdom of God; it also insists on something that is more difficult to believe, namely that repentance is *possible*. The possibility of repentance is postulated on an "open" universe in which neither persons nor nations need stumble in perpetuity, eternally trapped in their current outlooks, habits or perceptual prisms. The spiritual power at the core of reality makes new life chances possible. This is where the recently widely discussed "theology of hope" meets the core dilemma of the Turn East. As presented by its most eloquent interpreters, the theology of hope is not a fuzzy brand of religious utopianism. Nor is it a blind belief that some extraterrestrial being will intervene on humankind's behalf like a magic genie. Rather, theology of hope is based on the confidence that real change, genuine novelty and unprecedented newness *can* appear in human life, that indeed the cosmos itself is supportive of such change. Based on this foundational faith, I do not believe Americans are sentenced to grope forever in the grotesque light patterns emitted by the prism. People can begin again. Even "new birth" is possible.

The answer to the riddle of the distorting prism is not a stronger light—it is the dismantling of the prism. This will not be easy, because the prism of the competitive-consumer way of life is part of a larger edifice of social patterns and economic practices. It is the result of our allowing those institutions that live by profit, expansion and cash value to assume the seats of power and to dictate their modes of thought to everyone else. Jesus told the rich young inquirer he had to sell all his goods and give the money to the poor before he could even set foot on the path to the Kingdom of God. We should be careful not to universalize this command too glibly—yet surely there is a direct connection between our inability really to hear the Eastern teachings and our unwillingness to give up our personal and national quest for economic supremacy and military invulnerability. As a society, and often as individuals, we want to set our feet unswervingly toward enlightenment, but to keep a firm toehold on the securities of whatever privileges we have been able to garner. The contradiction is an impossible one. Although America *seems* receptive to Eastern spiritual teachings, it is receptive only up to a point. Just as repentance must *precede* entrance into the Kingdom, so the willingness to alter the very basis of our common life must precede our ability to hear, really to hear, what the East has to teach us. We will not hear until we change.

It may seem ironic, even contradictory, that I base my confidence on the eventual possibility of our hearing and learning from the East on what many will identify as a "Western" theological premise: the capacity of human beings, and even of human societies, to change. But I do not believe this need be contradictory. If the biblical belief that grace makes change possible is true at all, then it must surely include the possibility that Western people will be able to sacrifice their current confidence in production and performance and thus be inwardly prepared to hear what the East has to teach. For the truth is that just as, in the Buddhist teaching, egolessness and detachment are not merely ideas to be discussed, but discoveries, so the genuine possibility of seemingly impossible change (called "grace" by theologians) is not simply an article of belief, but something that must be experienced. It can be experienced, however, only by those who let go of their current survival tactics and open themselves to just that impossible possibility.

There is no contradiction in my idea that only the reality of grace can open the West to the East, because ultimately the "meeting of East and West" is not a matter of ideas at all. When it occurs at the level of ideas, the result is always either polemic and proselytizing or—what we now seem to have—premature synthesizing and superficial equating. We have now come to a time when the meeting must take place not in the realm of ideas but in the lives of actual persons living in real societies—that is, in the flesh. When that begins to happen, as I believe it can, then eventually the ideas will follow. "He that doeth the will of God shall know the doctrine."

10 The Myth of the Orient

During the summer of 1976 I returned to Naropa, again to offer a course on the "Life and Teachings of Jesus"—and to learn more about the Buddhist path. As soon as I arrived I began to notice changes, both in Naropa and in myself. At the opening faculty reception, Chogyam Trungpa shook my hand and asked, "How long can you stay with us this summer?" It was a perfectly hospitable welcome, but I also caught an intonation which I had not detected before: "you" and "us." Naropa was becoming more explicitly "Buddhist." I was an honored guest, as I had been the year before, but despite my year-old meditational practice, I was no more than a guest. Just as I had needed to adjust to being a practitioner of shamatha meditation who was, however, not a Buddhist, so the Buddhists had learned not to regard me as a prospective convert. The lines had become clearer all around.

I was not the only one who noticed the difference. The evidence of the clarification process was everywhere. Naropa was now administered by people who had all lived through years of Buddhist training and practice. Some had been sent by Chogyam Trungpa from Karmê Chöling, the study and meditation center which an acquaintance of mine had once dubbed "Buddhist bootcamp." It was clear that the process had been Trungpa's own decision. "We are not concerned with adapting . . ." he had told an interviewer a few months earlier, "but with handling the teaching here in a skillful way."

When Tibetans began to present Buddhism in this country, we did it in keeping with the people's mentality and language. As people understand it more and more, it begins to take a real traditional form. If we were to present all the heavy traditional stuff at the beginning, then all sorts of fascination with Tibetan culture and enlightenment would take place, and the basic message would be lost. So it is good to start with a somewhat free form and slowly tighten it up. (Trungpa, 1976)

It is significant that, according to this quotation, Trungpa had chosen this free form—followed by tightening up—approach not because he was afraid that beginning with the "heavy traditional stuff" would scare people away. Just the opposite. He did not want to fascinate people with Tibetan exotica and have them lose the basic message.

Whatever the reason, the most dramatic sign of the tightening up was the change in the format of Trungpa's two weekly lecture sessions. The "open space" I had enjoyed so much the year before, the two hours of informal conversation and idleness in the gym before lectures began, was now no more. Although Trungpa continued to appear two hours late, now the waiting period had been transformed into another sitting meditation session. Instead of the disorganized "beach scene" of the previous summer, now hundreds of students sat silently on black or yellow-and-orange *zafus* and meditated until the teacher appeared.

No doubt about it, Trungpa was tightening up. One rumor had it that the new toughness had been a result of the visit a few months earlier of His Holiness Gyalwa Karmapa, Trungpa's superior in the Kagyupa Order of Tibetan Buddhism, who had reportedly advised Trungpa to sharpen up the Buddhist identity of his Naropa operation. Other people denied the rumor, claimed that the Karmapa had been very pleased with Trungpa's work and insisted that Naropa's clearer Buddhist profile was a natural expression of Trungpa's own strategy for introducing Buddhism to America.

Whatever the reasons for the changes, I found that I appreciated them. The more explicit Buddhist atmosphere helped make the differences between the Buddhist and the Christian paths even plainer. It sharpened the dialogue. This in turn pressed me further along in the reappropriation of neglected aspects of my own tradition, a process which had begun with my first visit to Naropa. But the new particularity did not suit everyone. One young man who had spent two years studying with Trungpa and had considered himself well along the first stages of the Buddhist path confessed to me that he had been shocked and bewildered by the Karmapa's visit. After studying with Trungpa, who wears a sports coat and loves to use words like "terrific," "fantastic," and "bullshit," meeting the Karmapa, who speaks no English, wears traditional Tibetan garb, and puts much more emphasis on the ceremonial aspect of Buddhism than Trungpa himself does, was terribly disquieting. Indeed, while in America, the Karmapa staged the ancient Tibetan Black Crown ceremony, which features Tibetan horn and drum music, brocaded fabrics heaped on the Karmapa's throne and the displaying of a centuries-old Black Crown that is said to have the power of liberating people on sight. In the hours-long ceremony, the Karmapa places the crown on his own head and goes into a state of deep meditation called *samadhi*, after which he blesses some people, initiates others and gives out mantras and sacred words to devotees.

The Karmapa is unapologetically ritualistic in his approach. "In order to cleanse the sins and impurities of the body," he says through his British-born interpreter, "we use the yogic prostration practice. In order to cleanse the sins of the voice . . . we take the refuge of the Triple Gem and recite the one-hundred-syllable mantra of the Vajra Sattva. In order to cleanse the sins and impurities of the mind, tendencies which have been collected through countless lives and endless *kalpas* of time, we say mantras and bow to the Buddhas with a heartrending feeling of penitence for all the suffering we knowingly or unknowingly have caused others or inflicted on them." (Karmapa, 1976) One of his disciples put her attitude toward Karmapa as succinctly as it could be put. "To us," she said, "he *is* Buddha."

It is not surprising that some of Trungpa's fledgling followers were upset by their encounter with the Karmapa and the Black Crown ceremony. After listening for months to Trungpa's colloquial and often derisively antiritualistic lectures, meeting his superior must have come as something of a surprise. Some, of course, were fascinated and drawn deeper into the Vajrayana

Buddhist tradition. Some began to wonder if they had not made a mistake to embark on a path that now seemed to lead toward elaborate penitential rituals, prostrations and magic crowns. But I am sure Trungpa's strategy was correct and that the Karmapa's visit was well timed. Eventually those attracted to this version of the Buddhist path should understand clearly just how demanding and elaborate, in a sense, how "foreign," it is. This will separate the dilettantes from the disciples. It will prevent premature synthesizing and make it more possible for Buddhism to be presented in America as a genuinely *different* option, not as one more candidate for cultural cooptation.

Just before I left Naropa for the second time I was invited by the faculty to give a kind of farewell lecture. Speaking from the same stage from which Trungpa ordinarily lectures, I gave some reflections—as a Christian theologian—on what I had come to know of the Buddhist path. I welcomed the Buddhist teachers to America and wished them well in their efforts to introduce this venerable tradition here. But I warned them about the problem of the cultural prism, the pseudodetachment we already have, the danger that what appears to be a genuine receptivity to their ideas may be just the opposite. And I ended by warning them that Americans will never be able to hear the message the real Orient has for us so long as we keep a mythical Orient in our heads.

This last problem seems to me the most difficult one, the one that continues to make the new Orientalism more a peril than a promise. It is the fact that there are actually two "Orients." One is made of real people and real earth. The other is a myth that resides in the head of Westerners. One is an actual cultural area, stretching from India to Japan and from Mongolia to Singapore. The other is a convenient screen on which the West projects reverse images of its own deficiencies. This mythical Orient once consisted almost entirely of sages and fakirs, magical talismans and esoteric lore, serpents weaving to nasal flutes, infinite holiness, wisdom and inner peace. Recently this Western dream of an Eastern Xanadu has soured somewhat. It now includes some nightmare qualities: elusive guerrilla bands, teeming pools of population, swarming yellow hordes waving little red books and hypnotic cult leaders bent on brainwashing idealistic youngsters. The West's inner Orient accommodates both our fondest fantasies and our most gruesome fears. The Orient symbolizes both threat and promise in the imagination of the West, and the two elements feed on each other, like paradise and perdition.

Psychologists and theologians both know the myth-making inclinations of human beings, their tendency to invent a Beulah Land of perfection over the rainbow or beyond the blue horizon. In the Western psyche "the Indies" has always had more of a mythical than a geographical meaning. In Columbus' time the Indies meant not only India and Cathay (as China was called then); it also signified whatever it was that Europe lacked and sought. Was the West poor? To the East lay El Dorado, the landscape tiered with cities of gold. Was the West aging, failing in vigor? Somewhere in the East bubbled the miraculous fountain of youth. Was our religion corrupt and repressive? There, unspoiled natives dwelt in naked innocence, enjoying childlike pleasures and recognizing only the benevolent creator whose sacred writ was the ebb and flow of nature itself. Were our rulers stupid and arrogant? There, one could find the great Khan who always governed wisely and well, or the righteous realm of Prester John, the perfect priest king.

Why was it that Europe pushed eastward until it met itself on the other side? Undoubtedly commerce had much to do with it, and it surely is no coincidence that the European expansion into the Orient happened just as the early signs of capitalism were showing. But it was more than that. As J. W. Parry says in *The European Reconnaissance*, "If the search for India had been only a matter of balancing possible profit against financial and maritime risk, the decision to attempt it might have been still longer delayed; but the pull which India exerted on the European imagination was not commercial only." (Parry, 1968)

The "pull" of which Parry speaks may be the other side of an inner push, that restlessness which Augustine found in himself and which some theologians see in all souls, but which is probably more Western than universal. Parry himself says that the explorers of the Renaissance period were motivated not only by practical ends but also by "a search for Christian perfection." Though fifteenth-century Europe was assured, as he says, "of its possession of Christian revelation," it had reason to doubt whether its way of life was a very exemplary embodiment of that revelation. "For some, at least, of its spiritual and intellectual leaders," he continues, "perfection was not here, not now; it had existed long ago in time; it might be found again surviving far away in space."

The East, first as the "New World," then as the "Far East," is where Westerners have gone to convert, to conquer, to colonize, always driven by an inner disquietude. As Hernando Cortez said to the Aztecs when he landed, "We have a sickness of the soul for which gold is the only cure." But gold was obviously not the cure; why then has the search continued when, despite shiploads of bullion, no answer has been found to the soul sickness of the searcher? The question can never be answered satisfactorily, because myths cannot be refuted by facts, and human beings stubbornly persist in finding what they are looking for. Columbus died firm in the belief that the sandy Caribbean islands he had discovered were the outlying islands of India or Japan.

Throughout Western history this mythical Orient has had its cartographers and explorers just as the real Orient has. The human proclivity to see what one has been looking for is so strong that many travelers and traders who journeyed to the Orient also became elaborators of its myth. After Marco Polo and his brothers did actually visit China, they helped to perpetuate and embellish the Western legends about the East. Columbus, a good sailor, kept the myth of the Indies alive even when the facts were not very supportive. Cortez and Pizarro immortalized the fables of Mexico and Peru before destroying them. Any contemporary traveler to the Orient is so programmed by hundreds of years of image-making that his capacity to see what is actually there is much diminished.

Enterprising Orientals have learned, of course, how to show us what we want to see. Perceptive entrepreneurs, East and West, can now supply the pilgrim or tourist (the distinction between the two is seldom clear) with precisely the Orient he or she sets out to see. This same process happens everywhere. It is the "prepared environment syndrome." In parts of Africa guides have become skilled in leading inexperienced hunters on a safari that actually moves in a large circle and ends, after a few days, at a location where the guides knew there were some aging lions even before the trek began. Latin America innkeepers, realizing that most travelers long to return home and report that they avoided tourist traps and got close to the local people, have now constructed shelters that specifically cater to this anti-tourist taste. On the Rue Pigalle in Paris there stands a nightclub called Les Naturistes whose builders intentionally designed it and decorated it so that it would look exactly like a Hollywood movie version of a French nightclub. They did so because they had noticed that many Americans, their expectations shaped by films, tended to be disappointed by the genuine *boites de nuit.* Les Naturistes does a splendid business, not only with Americans but with Europeans whose introduction to what a nightclub looks like came first from a movie. It would be naïve indeed to suppose that the same prepared environment syndrome does not apply to the Oriental pagodas and ashrams Westerners visit. It applies especially to Oriental movements that set out to cultivate an American clientele. Reality imitates art, and institutions of religion are often shaped around images of what they are believed and hoped to be.

Who actually forges our images of the "mysterious East"? The truth is that they are not simply forged. They arise from deep needs in the Western psyche and are then polished, refined and distributed by writers, film-makers, and inventors of advertising copy. Rudyard Kipling, the Victorian poet, is perhaps the best example of the influential Oriental image polisher. Kipling wrote his poems and stories at the height of the power of the British Empire, and he left impressions and characters that still affect us. There was a time when nearly every English schoolboy, and many Americans as well, could recite at least a part of "Gunga Din"; that loyal water carrier who died taking a canteen to a British grenadier under fire was, according to one critic, the best known Indian in the West until Gandhi came on the scene.

Kipling is long since dead, the Empire in retreat, and the Victorian ethos dethroned. But songs reverberate after the singing is done and images linger when the stimulus is past. Kipling's India still retains a grip on the imagination of the West. This is not just because his plots and characters have appeared in all manner of films—*Gunga Din* alone was filmed three times in Hollywood—but also because Kipling captured the imaginary India that survives in the fantasy life of Westerners. Never a reliable guide to the real India, Kipling is the conjurer par excellence of that bundle of impressions the Western mind calls "India." These strange Orientals in Kipling's lines have something we lack. Ignorant, wily, elusive, intransigent they may be—perhaps even ungrateful and ferocious at times—but underneath they possess a purity we lack. The quest for perfection which J. H. Parry sees as the spark of Western colonialism remains alive in Kipling's attitude toward Her Majesty's heathen subjects. The myth says there is a place of perfection and it lies Somewhere Else. It is a myth that springs from hope.

Another part of the myth springs from fear. Orientals possess strange powers they could use against us. They are wily and malevolent, like another movie favorite, Dr. Fu Man-Chu. Of the two stereotypes, we strongly prefer Gunga Din. Him we can trust. After all, he earned the right to be praised as "a better man than I am" by dying in the service of the Queen of England. We like him ever so much more than Dr. Fu Man-Chu. Still it is not hard to see behind the Gunga Din image of the gentle, spiritually pristine Oriental a certain wishful thinking on the part of the English colonizer. Better a servile water carrier with a soul of gold than an angry Sepoy rebel with a black heart. Better a smiling meditator than a frowning Maoist.

What happens when history threatens to shatter the myth we hold of the Orient? How do our perceptions change when the Orient asserts an identity that does not conform to our image? The answer is that when reality threatens to engulf the myth, we cling to the myth more fiercely. Even Kipling knew that empires do not last forever. After singing about holding "dominion over palm and pine," he could remind us of the inevitable day when "all the pomp of yesterday" would be "One with Nineveh and Tyre." In decline as well as glory, empires retain a mythical attitude toward the colonial. As facts undermine the myth a painful ambivalence sets in. Tommy Atkins grudgingly respects Gunga Din while shooting at the latter's countrymen; and the Anglican missionary vaguely suspects that the Hindus may have valuable wisdom of their own even as he passes out Malayalam translations of the Book of Common Prayer. My point here is that Americans have inherited the same myth and are experiencing the same ambivalence, and we cannot understand the current massive interest in the spirituality of Asia unless we see it within the context of America's shrinking Asian "empire." Whatever their intentions, visiting gurus will be cast as religious versions of Dr. Fu Man-Chu or Gunga Din. They embody our fantasies of what Orientals *should* be like.

Empires must always deal with the religions of those societies they dominate. Sometimes they simply destroy them. Christians and Muslims seem to have favored this strategy. Sometimes they use the religions of their satraps for the purpose of dividing and dominating, as England did so adroitly for so long in India, or they may try to emulate as the Romans did the Greeks. Always they distort indigenous faiths in one way or another. Eventually the colonizers begin to realize the enormity of what they have done, and the guilt begins to tincture hope and engender fear.

The Aztecs of Mexico never quite forgave themselves for their ruthless suppression of the Toltecs, and they were always a little frightened at the prospect of a Toltec uprising. They admired Toltec culture, added Toltec ancestors to their elaborate family genealogies, and integrated Toltec deities into their own pantheon as smoothly as the Romans once appropriated the Greek pantheon shortly after conquering the Greek states. Still, the Aztecs always feared that the legendary Toltec god-king Quetzalcoatl would return one day to take vengeance and reestablish his throne. This fear, incidentally, made them extremely vulnerable to the Spanish conquistadores who were first mistakenly seen as the exiled god's avatars, and who were more than willing to sit in for Quetzalcoatl if it would help them defeat the Aztecs.

In view of these distinguished precedents it seems less than surprising that the American fascination with Eastern spirituality should have begun in the nineteenth century just as our belief in manifest destiny began to reach out toward the Pacific —and has culminated just as our country's power has crested and begun to recede in Asia. The dominator gets rid of his guilt by making the dominated holier, wiser or more virtuous than himself.

Our current admiration for what we think are Oriental religions, whatever else it may be, is one way of coping with a bad conscience. Unable to slow down the swift Westernization of some parts of Asia, bewildered by the power and independence of other parts, we try to console ourselves with thoughts of how simple and virtuous the Asians really are. Two centuries ago Marie Antoinette and her court attributed the same virtues to unlettered shepherds. She wore a peasant's cap and bade her courtiers dress in silks cut to give a pastoral impression. She distributed shepherds' crooks to the court and ordered everyone to sing country ditties while lounging around carefully built replicas of rustic cottages. Our interest in the Orient today has something of the same quality. While inundating the East with American products, yet sensing vaguely that we can no longer dominate parts of Asia, we begin to dress in their costumes and help ourselves to their religions—conveniently packaged for Western consumption.

The final paradox is that few Easterners ever claim to be able to save the West. Frequently they deny having any interest in doing so even if they could. They rarely send missionaries here and they accept Western novices with reluctance. Although the Westernized versions of Eastern faiths do often claim to bring salvation to the West, at this point they betray the spirit of their sources and actually worsen the Western dilemma by advertising more than they can deliver. The spiritual crisis of the West will not be resolved by spiritual importations or individual salvation. It is the crisis of a whole civilization, and one of its major symptoms is the belief that the answer must come from Elsewhere. Thus the crisis can be met only when the West sets aside myths of the Orient and returns to its own primal roots.

An old Zen story tells of a pilgrim who mounted his horse and crossed formidable mountains and swift rivers seeking a famous roshi in order to ask him how to find true enlightenment. After months of searching, the pilgrim located the teacher in a cave. The roshi listened to the question and said nothing. The seeker waited. Finally after hours of silence, the roshi looked at the steed on which the pilgrim had arrived and asked the pilgrim why he was not looking for a horse instead of enlightenment. The pilgrim responded that obviously he already had a horse. The roshi smiled and retreated to his cave.

Eventually the spiritual disciplines of the Orient will make a profound contribution to our consciousness and our way of life. Some day, somewhere, we will hear the message the East has for us. But we can only begin to know the real Orient when we are willing to let go of the mythical one. And we can only begin to hear the message of the Oriental religious traditions when we are willing to confront the inner dislocations in our own civilizations which caused us to invent the myth of the East in the first place; and when we are willing to do that, we may realize that what we are seeking so frantically elsewhere may turn out to be the horse we have been riding all along.

11 Toward a Spirituality of the Secular

We need an authentic contemporary form of spirituality. We must find it, I believe, in our own tradition, not somewhere else. But where do we begin to look for it? In the Buddhist spiritual path the whole lineage of masters through whom the dharma has been conveyed is honored, but the most important masters are the founders of the line at one end and one's own master at the other—the classical source and the living teacher through whom the dharma comes to me. In the meditation hall of the Boston Dharmadatu, for example, where I sometimes go to meditate, there are four prominently displayed pictures. One is of the Buddha. One is of Avilokitsvara, the founder of the lineage. Another is the master of the current teacher; and the last is of the current master himself. I believe this same principle of geneological selectivity also applies in Christianity. Next to Jesus and the first Christians, it is our direct mentors in the faith who play the most significant role. We should honor these godfathers and godmothers more than we usually do. Not only honor them but, in a sense, become their disciples. They constitute the critical link between ourselves and our past. Thus I believe that as late twentieth-century Christians trying to work out a viable spirituality, there are two principal historical sources to which we should look. They are the earliest period of our history and the most recent, the first Christian generations and the generation just before us.

I believe we should look principally to the primal sources and to the Christians nearest us, because the ransacking of other periods for help in working out a contemporary spirituality soon becomes either antiquarian or downright misleading. The

Catholic nostalgia for medieval culture—shorn of pogroms and plagues, of course—seems to be fading now. So does the Protestant idealization of an allegedly more godly small-town Currier and Ives America. It is just as well. We cannot recycle either of these highly mythicized eons for our own spirituality today. When we try, we soon recognize that the saints of those and other in-between eras were different from us in ways that make it virtually impossible to turn to them as models. They were saints, in fact, because they successfully shaped a mode of religious existence that reverberated with *their* cultures as ours must with ours.

When we study the first few generations of Christians, however, we feel a strange shock of recognition. They are different from us too, but to our surprise we find we have more in common with them than we expected. The first practitioners of the Christ dharma, for example, lived in a pre-Christian culture. We live in a post-Christian culture. They had little to go on except the Law and the Prophets and their own experience of Jesus and the Spirit. They did not even have the New Testament, since they were, in fact, creating it. We are also feeling our way with few available guidelines. Since no one else has ever had to live out the Christian vision in a culture that was once allegedly "Christian" and no longer is, we must rely mainly on the same sources they did. They constituted the first generations after Christ. We are the first generations after Christendom. They were a tiny minority in a none-too-hospitable world. We are swiftly attaining the same status. They had to hammer out what they believed in the face of a cascade of varying religious world views that swirled not just around their congregations but through them. So must we. They worked on the task of defining the Christ dharma with what appears in retrospect to have been amazing skill and subtlety. They boldly absorbed religious practices and ideas—eucharist, baptism, logos philosophy—from their environment with what many theologians today would reject as blatant syncretism. We are free to be equally bold. They also drew lines and made distinctions that others recoil from today as arrogant, but they did so because they wanted their bewildered contemporaries to hear the Christ dharma with unmistakable clarity. They were convinced it was "good news," the best news, in fact, that anyone could possibly hear. We have the same responsibility—to make sure that what people hear is the gospel and not a culturally disfigured caricature. At no time in the nineteen centuries since Jesus has the Christian movement had more to learn than we do from the early formative years. Those wavering backsliders and ecstatic dreamers of Corinth, Rome, and Philippi are our brothers and sisters in a more important sense than are all the popes and preachers in between. Any authentic post-modern spirituality must begin by going back to the sources.

This does not mean we can neglect the long and variegated history of Christianity that stretches from the age of the Apostles and their followers to the beginning of our time. We need to know this period. But I think we should read it more as a cautionary tale than as a treasure house of available inspiration. We Christians today need to understand our history much as a compulsive neurotic needs to understand his—in order to see where we veered off, lost genuine options, glimpsed something we were afraid to pursue, or denied who we really are. Indeed, the most therapeutic accounts of our history for us today may not be the official ones, which sound defensive and self-serving, and often read like the religious equivalents of campaign biographies. What we need more are the neglected and repressed histories of what happened to the Montanists and the Cathari, to the Hussites and the Waldensians, to those who were branded as witches, heretics and schismatics. We need to reabsorb these people into our history today much as a neurotic person needs to reclaim parts of the self that have been denied or projected onto others. The outcasts of our history were burned or banished—at the time the social equivalent to repressing and projecting—but they have more to teach us now than their orthodox judges do. Their vision may have been too early for their time, but it is not too early for ours.

A trite adage avers that we must learn from history or suffer the pain of repeating it. The fact is that religious people often seem to read their history fired by a blind determination to repeat it at all costs. But it need not be so. We should study our Christian history not to suffuse it with sanctity but to discover how much of it has been excrescence and grotesquerie, to realize that we—like those earliest People of the Way—have got to start all over, or almost. If we are going to have a spirituality for our time, then we cannot borrow it from the East or resuscitate it from the past. We will have to forge it ourselves with the materials at hand, just as they did.

To some, the challenge to shape a spirituality that is at once biblical and contemporary will sound impossible of attainment, a herculean task in an age without heroes. But the nub of what I have just said about starting over is not so much that we *must* as that we *can*. Imagine a contemporary Christian spirituality rooted in the Hebrew prophets, the Christ dharma and the creativity of the early Christians. How much spurious encumbrance and religious nostalgia it could cut through. If we need not stagger into the twenty-first century dragging the full impedimenta of nineteen previous centuries, all things become possible. Then we can look to St. Thomas Aquinas (whose books, after all, were publicly burned by his contemporaries), St. Francis (who was nearly excommunicated), Martin Luther (who was), more as explorers who went ahead by first returning to the sources. We honor them today not by mimicking Franciscan piety or perpetuating Thomist or Lutheran theology, but by returning to the same sources and risking the same willingness to innovate. We should be careful, above all, not to sanctify this or that allegedly golden period of the Christian past into another storied realm of Prester John, removed from us not by space but by time. For Christians, just as the Kingdom of God never was situated somewhere else in space, it also never lies in some bygone era in time. It is coming, and in the midst of us, or it is nowhere at all.

I have said that in order to work out a spirituality for our post-modern times we need to come to grips with two generations of Christians, the first one and our own. Both are crucial. From the first Christians we can learn how to be born again, how to flourish as a fringe group, how to use whatever is at hand to celebrate the Spirit, feed the widows, and make known the Christ. But beyond that, the early Christians cannot teach us very much else. As we avoid mythicizing other periods of history, we should also spare the first Christians this fate. We have little to learn from them, for example, about dislodging ensconced power, taming the atom, preventing the poisoning of the sea, or how to talk with life on other galaxies. They have less than nothing to teach us, it would seem, about the proper role of women, the place of slaves, and some other matters. Like us, they were fallible and finite. They made mistakes we need not repeat. But, unlike anyone else, they were there when it started; so it is to them we must go in order to start again. They teach us not by *what* they did but by *how* they did it—with serenity and the zestful conviction that they could risk untried stratagems because God would survive their mistakes. The Christians of the New Testament period remind us that we have the freedom to create an authentic contemporary form of spirituality. For the concrete shape of that spirituality, however, we must turn to each other and to our immediate predecessors in this first post-Christian century, the earliest post-Christendom Christians. Who are they?

For each of us, the list of near-contemporaries who have nourished our spirituality will be different. But I believe there is a growing consensus about a few figures to whom all, or nearly all, of us are drawn as our own gurus, as the first generation of post-modern Christians, whose exemplary lives and teachings help us eke out our own way of being. When I returned from Naropa for the last time, grateful for what I had learned but certain that my journey would now wend westward, I found myself turning to some of these gurus, or at least to their books, since some of them are already dead.

The first contemporary I turned to in my own attempt to construct a workable spirituality was Dietrich Bonhoeffer. This may come as no surprise, since Bonhoeffer, like myself, was a pastor and a theological writer. But there are others who fill this description. Why Bonhoeffer in particular? Maybe because he was a twentieth-century man par excellence, and yet a man of deep faith. The elegant, brilliant—perhaps even somewhat conceited—scion of a notable aristocratic family in Berlin, Bonhoeffer was a world traveler, a lover of the arts, a connoisseur of vintage wines and string quartets. An admirer of Gandhi, he nevertheless was able to sacrifice his philosophical pacifism in order to join the plot to assassinate Hitler, an act for which he was hanged in Flossenbürg concentration camp in April 1945, hours before the camp was liberated by the advancing American army.

Bonhoeffer speaks to my search for a contemporary spirituality because he too returned to the sources, the New Testament itself, and came to read it as an invitation to begin again. His *Letters and Papers from Prison* sketch in barest outline the dream of a Gospel freed at last from the remnants of obsolete metaphysics and constrictive pietism. Bonhoeffer tried until his dying day, although never successfully, to find a spirituality that would enable him to live in a world in which, as he put it, God had allowed himself to be edged out, but Christ could be met "at the center" where earthy life is thickest and most worldly. Bonhoeffer is an indispensable guru for those of us who, as he said, need to "live before God as though God did not exist"—which is what it must mean in part to be a Christian in the late twentieth century. His ideas of "anonymous Christianity" and "secret discipline," his reliance on a cadre of compatriots and his adamant refusal to let God be used to make up for human weakness or ignorance—all provide us with the building blocks we need to assemble the spirituality he never lived to develop himself.

Along with Bonhoeffer, the second guru I have turned to most often is that stubbornly indigestible Frenchwoman, Simone Weil. Roughly the contemporary of Bonhoeffer, Weil grew up in an educated if not a privileged family. Like him she was also raised on the classics but came later to yearn for nothing more than to serve God among the godless. As it happened, Weil's entry into the "godless world" was different from Bonhoeffer's and took her to a different kind of prison—the Renault automobile factory. But while working there she learned, as he did in the cellblock at Tegel, about affliction, courage and cowardice, and the tiny but infinitely valuable joys fellow prisoners and co-workers can share with one another. Like Bonhoeffer, Simone Weil hated the boundary the church had erected between believers and nonbelievers. Bonhoeffer dismantled the wall by insisting that the "true church" is nothing else than the world, claimed by God and inhabited by Christ. But Simone was born Jewish, raised a pagan and became a quasi-Marxist. She did not really have to go anywhere to be in the godless world; she was already there. Consequently, for Simone Weil, it was her refusal to be baptized into the church she believed in which signified her conviction that the Christ she loved dwelt also among scoffers and sinners.

It seems that all our post-modern gurus hold in common a firm conviction that to encounter the holy today one must move deeper *into* the "godless" world, not away from it. For all of them the narrow road to the Kingdom of God leads through the terrestrial city. No one has thought out this dimension of modern spirituality better than Amos Wilder in his essay on the "lay mystery" in which he says:

> Is it not true that Christianity has a need of recurrent baptism in the secular, in the human, to renew itself . . . to be saved over and over again from a spurious and phantom Christ? . . . Theology and witness today will be impoverished unless they take account of the secular man in all his dynamics; of the lay mystery that gives evidence of itself precisely in a desacralized world. (Wilder, 1969)

Dietrich Bonhoeffer and Simone Weil died within a year of each other. Neither ever read Wilder's words. But both dramatize how right he is. Both represent the rebaptism of the holy in the secular, a dawning awareness of the mystery that evidences itself in the desacralized world. Their paths into that mystery were different. Bonhoeffer's took him into the dark demiworld of conspiracy and espionage, and eventually to the gallows. Weil's took her into the often petty and acrimonious world of French intellectualism, and then to an early death in England caused in part by her refusal, though she was ill, to eat more than was permitted to her countrymen in occupied France. Both, however, died determined to share fully in whatever it means to embrace life in a century that believes it has left God behind, yet feels a hunger for a holiness that no churchly provision seems to feed. Both, from different sides, refused to allow the church wall to cut them off from a world where they believed Christ is present among the least likely.

There are other immediate forerunners of our own generation. My own hagiography includes one doughty octogenarian, Dorothy Day, the founder of the Catholic Worker movement, herself a pacifist and anarchist. Dorothy started her adult life by purposely getting arrested in New York City on Saturday nights so that she could share the tank with the prostitutes. She got herself in jail again about twenty years ago by calmly refusing to crawl into an air-raid shelter during a test alert. Her most recent brush with the authorities came when she sat serenely on a picket line with Mexican-American farmworkers in California and sweetly refused to move when ordered. On the other side of the violence/nonviolence spectrum, my calendar of saints includes Father Camilo Torres-Restrepo. Torres is the Colombian priest-sociologist who tried to organize a united people's political movement in his country in the 1960s, failed, and finally abandoned the effort to join a band of armed guerrillas in the hills. He was killed a few weeks afterward in a skirmish with the army. His body was never recovered. The authorities no doubt wanted to prevent a cult from growing up around his remains. Their caution was probably justified, for already a popular Latin American song declares that "where Camilo Torres fell, there sprung up a cross, not of wood but of light."

It might seem strange at first to include both Dorothy Day the pacifist and Camilo Torres the guerrilla in a single list of exemplars of present-day spirituality. But it should not be. What Dorothy and Camilo share, in addition to a certain personal quality of intensity modulated by irony, is the recognition that the world has taken the place of the Wilderness as the classical place for testing and purification. Though they might not have approved of each other's methods, and though they came from different social strata (Torres-Restrepo remains one of Colombia's most aristocratic families), still I suspect Dorothy and Camilo would have sensed a strong cord between them. Both had a commitment to the struggle for bread, spiced by a winning tolerance for the weaknesses of the flesh, even in themselves. Dorothy Day bore a child out of wedlock. Camilo is said to have enjoyed the companionship of women in a manner that did not seem commensurate with his vows of celibacy, at least to some of his acquaintances. In other words, both Dorothy Day and Camilo Torres broke from the cloying custom of identifying piety with moralism. They both felt that personal holiness is a wrestling match with the powers of evil in high places, and that this duel must be fought today eye to eye with monstrous corporate forces. Here is the indispensable insight any genuine contemporary spirituality must incorporate. It is the lay mystery.

I could add more names to my list of contemporary gurus. Martin Luther King has been idolized too soon by many (his birthday is already a legal holiday in some states) and discredited too quickly by others. But those who were stirred by his preaching and followed him willingly through the streets and into the jails know that he had begun to represent an engaging example of being fully Christian and fully immersed in both the joy and the pain of the urban world. Other politically committed Christians come to mind, such as Chief Albert Luthuli and Bishop Helder Câmara. But for most Americans—black or white—King still seems closer and more credible. And his assassination at the age of thirty-nine reminds everyone that modern discipleship still exacts its price.

Sometimes as I immerse myself in the lives and writings of these recent Christian voyagers I think about those writers on "spirituality" who are constantly exhorting us to cultivate the habit of reading devotional literature. They may be right, but the problem is that material published for such purposes today is almost universally admitted to be indescribably bad. Maybe these men and women I have just been discussing are in fact the ones whose lives and words should become our "devotional reading" today. There is an essential link between a style of spirituality and the kind of literature that feeds that style. The trouble is that most allegedly "devotional" literature today is actually a kind of religious pornography. This is true in a very literal sense. The pornography of sex and violence qualifies as pornography because it presents sex and violence unrelated to the concrete lives and circumstances of recognizable human beings. It is faceless. But so is much of the ostensibly pious literature of our day. Here, as elsewhere, we would do well to avoid the pornography (which like all porn eventually becomes tiresome) and steep ourselves instead in the "Lives of the Saints"—our own saints.

The Kings and Weils and Bonhoeffers and Days feed us today for more than one reason. First of all they are not simple shepherds, fisherfolk or unlettered peasants. They are urban, post-modern people like us. They know about Darwin, Freud, Marx, contraception, imperialism and ennui. Their lives span not some idealized past, but our own fractured times. They carry all the alleged handicaps to belief that we do, yet they still manage to be Christians. Not only does the Christ dharma come to us through them, but the temporal proximity of their lives to ours makes the gospel more credible. Watching them, we realize that we must now find a way to live faithfully in a world that is already in some measure different from theirs, in which another generation will look to us for credible models of Christian existence.

It is important to realize that to learn from our forerunners we need not always agree with them. I cannot accept whole sections in some of their writings. Bonhoeffer, for example, often seems to me never to have shed his aristocratic hauteur, even in prison. Simone Weil occasionally let her spirited criticisms of the history of Israel cross the border into something close to antisemitism. I have other difficulties with Dorothy Day and Martin Luther King. But our disagreements with our godparents need not prevent us from learning from them. Also, we ought to remember that each of these twentieth-century disciples had a singular style. We learn from each of them individually, not as mere representatives of a vague construct such as "contemporary spirituality." Still, when one examines their lives and writings with care, some common threads do emerge, and these also help us in our quest. For example, of the exemplary figures I have mentioned probably only Simone Weil would have been conversant with the Buddhist belief that the essential pillars of any spiritual path must include dharma (teaching), *sangha* (community), and Buddha or guru (the teacher or model). But the more I learn about the people I have named above, the more the presence of these three pillars becomes evident. It is here that my own search for a viable spirituality intersects with theirs. I know that I, like them, need a clear teaching I can believe with both head and heart, a dharma. Also I, like them, need a company of trusted comrades who will chasten, criticize and support me, be there when I need them, go away when I don't want them, and expect the same from me. This is what the Buddhists call the *sangha*. And, as is evident from this chapter, I need *provisional* gurus, partial exemplars, models not so much to emulate as to argue with, learn from and—eventually—discard.

Does everyone need all three components? Some people may be able to get along today without one or more of the three. There are some, for example, who seem to thrive on dharma alone. They read Auden or Eliot, or Tillich or C. S. Lewis, depending on their tastes, and seem to need *sanghas* or gurus only in very minor ways. Their worship is often confined to Christmas Eve and Easter Sunday plus periodic feast days and *rites de passage*. These Christian intellectuals are an imposing breed, but their spirituality seems a little airy to me. Personally, I cannot survive as a Christian on pure dharma alone.

Another species of contemporary Christian relies mainly on the liturgy or congregation but seems generally untroubled by the question of what message this medium is conveying. Like the Sufi dancers I mentioned earlier, who did not know—or care much about—the meanings of the Arabic words they were chanting, there are *sangha* Christians who seem genuinely uninterested in the content of the dharma except in the most conventional terms. These are the people who can lose themselves in the mass, soar with real fervor into Bach anthems or traditional prayers, or give of themselves unsparingly in social-action projects, but whose eyes assume a glazed quality when asked to tell anyone why. Again, I am not denigrating this communal-liturgical mode of spirituality. There are times in the history of any religion—and this may be such a time—when the dharma may seem confused and opaque but the community of concern goes on, sharing the uncertainty but sharing nonetheless. *Sangha* spirituality should not be viewed with contempt by the more content-oriented. In our lonely era especially, when so many people are so starved for friendship, *sangha* without dharma must be expected. But for me, as indispensable as a liturgical community is, it is not enough.

Finally, there is a form of spirituality that survives without either *sangha* or dharma but relies entirely on the one-to-one dyad. Let us call it "guru spirituality." It is less familiar than the other two because it has, by its very nature, become ever less institutionalized and therefore less visible. It consists in the spiritual direction given by one person to another in relationships ranging from single counseling sessions to extended psychoanalysis. For some people it is all they ever get by way of spiritual direction and nurture. We often hear today about the similarity between what a good guru and a skilled therapist can do for a person. There is much truth in the comparison. But there is much that is misleading in it too. In our culture the therapist operates, at least ostensibly, without either a dharma or a *sangha*. Even if his clients constitute a group, as they do in some forms of counseling, the group usually has few other characteristics of a *sangha;* and if there is a teaching it is some mixture of psychological theory and popular humanism that the best practitioners concede will just not do as real dharma.

Once more, it is important for dharma and *sangha* Christians not to be too severe with those who rely on some westernized kind of guru in the person of a counselor or analyst. Since our own religious tradition, apart from a few scattered novice masters, is so deficient in providing spiritual directors, it is not surprising that hundreds of thousands of people have turned, often at great personal expense and sacrifice, to their secular equivalents.

But again, it is just not enough—at least for me, and I suspect for most people. All the most effective counselors or analysts can do is to help their clients to be able to make decisions on their own. They help bring about a condition in which the unconscious underbrush is hacked away and the person is ready to start making choices unimpeded by invisible encumbrances. But this is just the moment when both the Word and the Sacramental Community have their greatest importance. A spirituality reduced to the master-disciple or therapist-client scale is surely better than nothing at all. But because it lacks both dharma and *sangha*, it cannot suffice, not in the long run.

What, then, can our near contemporary spiritual masters teach us about *sangha*, dharma, and guru, the three pillars of any spirituality? To answer this question we have to probe their lives as well as their writings, for none of them dealt with this question in just these terms. But even a cursory examination of how they lived will quickly reveal the pillars.

Sangha: No one who reads Dorothy Day's column "On Pilgrimage" can possibly miss noticing that it reads almost like a travel diary and address book:

> It is a beautiful, sunny day, midwinter in Tivoli. No wind to chill the bones, and the children, those who are not napping, are out playing on the lawn. Only Tanya goes to school and she will be home soon.
>
> The men are hauling wood down from the hillside, clearing out dead trees, and Chuck Matthei and Charles Goodding have brought loads of driftwood from the Hudson. . . . There is no ice yet, but I just saw a wagon load of driftwood, tree trunks and logs go by the window towed by John Filliger's tractor. . . . The repairs of the ceiling were accomplished by two students from Iowa, who spent their strength and the three hundred dollars donated by their friends and by Jean's parents, Al and Monica Hagan. . . . (Day, 1976)

The rest of this column is studded, as are all her books and columns, with the names of people, living and dead, and places, near and far. For Dorothy Day the mystical body of Christ is not very mystical at all. It is not even "The Catholic Worker" as an organization. It is the Joe's and Marcia's and Gordon's she visits, eats with, travels with, and prays for. Dorothy Day's spirituality is utterly dependent on a *sangha*. Without it, her life and witness would be unimaginable.

The same centrality of the *sangha* principle holds for Bonhoeffer. During the early Hitler years, Bonhoeffer was deprived by the Nazis of any opportunity to teach or preach legally; so he organized an underground seminary. But, unlike a university theological school, Bonhoeffer's seminary-in-exile in Finkenwalde was a closely knit household where students and professors lived together and shared everything, including the constant danger of a Gestapo raid (which eventually came, causing the closing of the school). After the dispersal of the Finkenwalde brotherhood, Bonhoeffer expended long hours composing letters by the dozens to the students and colleagues who had been drafted into the army. But he did not find such companionship again until his brother-in-law, Hans von Dohnanyi, initiated him into the secret cabal that was planning to kill Adolf Hitler. Bonhoeffer's arrest on another charge in April 1943 deprived him of these friends too. It was then that, much to his own surprise, he began to discover a *sangha* among both the political prisoners and the common offenders with whom he shared the gray routine of incarceration. In his *Life Together*, based on the Finkenwalde years, Bonhoeffer writes explicitly about the indispensability of a disciplined supportive circle. Though he is sometimes seen as a lonely and isolated man—which he often was—I still believe Bonhoeffer's spirituality could have emerged only from his *sangha*.

In the individualistic religious climate of our time we have something to learn from the fact that all the godparents I have mentioned attached a great importance to *sangha*. Martin Luther King's Southern Christian Leadership Conference multiplied local branches during the 1960s and provided a web of confidantes and phone numbers for hundreds of civil-rights activists at a time when official church bodies often looked askance at pickets and demonstrators. And it supplied a *sangha* for King himself. Only Simone Weil, among our godparents, seems to be the exception. Although attracted by the Catholic Church, she never joined it. In fact she resisted joining anything. My own conviction is, however, that this resistance to organizations is not an expression of Weil's rejection of the idea of *sangha* but rather a mark of the earnestness with which she sought it. In her little book *The Mysticism of Simone Weil*, Marie-Magdeleine Davy attributes the striking lack of any corporate quality in Weil's spirituality to her sometimes overly zealous pursuit of self-denial and solitude. Weil often consciously deprived herself of just what she wanted most, not to gain some other goal but in order to share in the historic suffering of humankind. Her rejection of organizations was both a self-discipline and a criticism of the artificiality of the solidarity proffered. "She rejected [the collective]," Davy writes, "with a violence which is only explicable through the purity and intransigence of her search for the holy. . . ." She was such a perfectionist that she never found the friendship she so obviously longed for. (Day, 1951)

Dharma: The most striking thing to me about our godparents' understanding of the Teaching is that no one of them is a "liberal." They all have more or less orthodox theologies, so much so, in fact, that this makes them appear radical in light of the dominant interest of modern theology in modernizing and accommodating.

Bonhoeffer, for example, was often considered a maverick by his scholarly colleagues. Like Karl Barth, the leading "neo-orthodox" theologian of his time, whom Bonhoeffer admired—though with reservations—he rejected most of the liberal German theologians' efforts to accommodate Christianity to modern culture. Thus, in one of his better-known letters, Bonhoeffer sharply criticized Rudolf Bultmann, a fellow theologian, for the "typical liberal reduction process," he used in interpreting the New Testament. Bonhoeffer asserted that he was of the view that " . . . the full content, including the mythological concepts, must be maintained." The New Testament "is not a mythological garbing of the universal truth; this mythology (resurrection and so on) is the thing itself—but the concepts must be interpreted in such a way as not to make religion a precondition of faith. . . . Not until that is achieved," Bonhoeffer concludes, "will, in my opinion, liberal theology be overcome." (Bonhoeffer, 1967)

Although Bonhoeffer often seems to be criticizing his colleagues for being too timid, what he really was striving for was a devastating rejection of all conventional Christianity, a rejection based on a bold reappropriation of the most thoroughgoing reading of the Incarnation. His point was that since God had already joined the human race irrevocably in Christ, no further accommodation was needed. The ultimate accommodation, so to speak, had already taken place. Bonhoeffer's ultra-orthodoxy made him a radical among the liberals.

Exactly the same can be said, in their own ways, for both

Dorothy Day and Simone Weil. Dorothy Day's discomfort with some aspects of the Vatican Two "*aggiornamento*" is well known. She has never advocated women priests, a vernacular Mass, or even a rethinking of infallibility. It is said that she once scolded Father Daniel Berrigan for not treating the host with sufficient deference during a war-protest Mass. She describes herself as an angry but loyal daughter of the church, and she has been able to coax so many people toward a more radical social stance in part because she has remained so conservative in other respects. Like Bonhoeffer and Simone Weil, who was also no modernist, Dorothy Day demonstrates how a genuinely orthodox dharma can provide a more cutting, critical perspective on the world than a grossly accommodated one. Our other godparents have discovered the same thing. Even Martin Luther King, who came closer to being a liberal theologian in some of his writings than the others do, was at his best when his preaching and protest were grounded in the Hebrew prophets and the spiritual tradition of the Black Baptist church.

Guru: Finally, all our immediate forerunners had a strong sense of the role of the spiritual friend, the Christian *kalyanamitra*. Dorothy Day hardly writes a paragraph without mentioning the name of Peter Maurin, her own teacher and example. She not only looked to him for guidance and inspiration while he was alive, but returns to his *Easy Essays* and his memory now that he is dead. Simone Weil carried on a lifelong correspondence with the people she met whom she considered her spiritual guides. Bonhoeffer's most memorable book is not a book at all but a posthumous collection of the letters he sent from prison, many of them to his lifelong friend and colleague Eberhard Bethge.

Throughout the *Letters and Papers from Prison* Bonhoeffer reveals the trust and confidence he feels for Bethge. "They keep on telling me," he writes from his cell on April 30, 1944, "that I am 'radiating so much peace around me,' and that I am 'ever so cheerful.' Very flattering, no doubt, but I'm afraid I don't always feel like that myself. You would be surprised and perhaps disturbed if you knew how my ideas on theology are taking shape. This is where I miss you most of all, for there is no one else who could help me so much to clarify my own mind." On

June 5 he writes, "I don't see any point in my not telling you I have occasionally felt the urge to write poetry. You are the first person I have mentioned it to. So I'm sending you a sample, because I think it's silly to have any secrets from you. . . ." Other similar passages appear in letter after letter. Bethge was Bonhoeffer's *kalyanamitra,* though neither man knew the word.

Simone seems to have placed the same kind of confidence, at least for a while, in her adviser and correspondent Father Perrin. "I owe you an immense debt of gratitude. Sometimes, through my friendship, I have given some human beings an easy opportunity of wounding me. Some have taken advantage of it, either frequently or infrequently, some consciously, some unconsciously, but all have done it at one time or another. But you never."

Martin Luther King, Jr., was more fortunate than most. He grew up in a tradition in which the role of spiritual master still obtains, at least for preachers. It continues in the apprenticeship practice of the black churches, the custom by which aspiring young pastors work closely with an older pastor, not just learning how to preach but also being schooled in a religious way of life. All of our predecessors in the faith had their gurus or, more importantly, they knew how to discover the *kalyanamitra* in friends and co-workers, how to seek personal guidance and criticism not only from books, but also from loving persons. We need to do the same.

Where does this leave me in my personal quest for a spiritual path and discipline today? My goal is summed up in a quotation from one of my oldest teachers, Professor Emeritus Amos Wilder. "If we are to have any transcendence today," writes Wilder, in the essay on the lay mystery to which I alluded earlier, " . . . it must be in and through the secular. . . . If we are to find any grace it is to be found in the world and not overhead. . . . " I think Wilder is right and that to uncover this "lay mystery" I need a "worldly" form of spirituality—one that includes a *group* of actual flesh-and-blood human beings who will nourish me without extricating me from society. I need a *gospel* that makes sense not of some special religious realm but of the actual day-to-day world I live in. And I need guides, *kalyanamitras*—both living and dead—to whom

I can apprentice myself. In my case the *sangha* is a struggling little church in my neighborhood, a place where I must contend with younger and older people some of whose views I appreciate and others of whose ideas I find intolerable. The music is often stirring, sometimes off key. The preaching is uneven. There is never enough money for the oil, despite numerous potluck suppers. How often I have been tempted to jettison this all-too-human little freckle on the Body of Christ and stay home on Sunday with better music (on the hi-fi) and better theology (from the bookshelf). But I do not. A voice within me keeps reminding me that I need these fallible human confreres, whose petty complaints never quite overshadow the love and concern underneath. This precarious little local church may not be the ideal Christian *sangha* for our time, though it has done more to become one than many other parishes have. Still, it exists. It is where Word becomes flesh, and it offers something of what a *sangha* should. I do not believe any modern Christian, whether a returnee from the East or not, can survive without some such grounding in a local congregation. Although this may require vast patience and tenacity, I see no other way it can be done. "One Christian," as Péguy said, "is no Christian."

As for the Christian dharma today, I have already indicated my decision to focus on the biblical roots. This is just what I do. When I was invited to teach the one course on Christianity at the Naropa Institute, I consciously decided to make it a course on Jesus and the beginnings of Christianity. I chose this topic as much for myself as for my students. I still believe there is no "spiritual reading" that can compare with Isaiah, Amos, Mark, and John, especially when they are read in tandem with the diaries of our contemporary saints. Admittedly, in concentrating on the biblical dharma as normative, there are serious problems today. One is residual American fundamentalism, which distorts the Bible into a magical oracle. The other is a kind of arid scholarship that details every critical theory about a text but never asks what it would mean to live by it. My struggle with the dharma will continue to concentrate on the sources themselves and on their most recent appropriations. I strongly suspect that people who are looking elsewhere will eventually come to this view too.

Finally, in my search for gurus, for Christian versions of the *kalyanamitra,* I turn to whoever can help: to the books of the "saints" I have discussed earlier in this chapter; to the brothers at the Benedictine monastery where I make a retreat twice a year; to the Buddhist meditation instructors who still patiently help me with my laggardly sitting practice, even though they know I will never become one of them; to a psychoanalytic counselor who mixes Freud with Buber and episodically but firmly prevents me from deceiving myself too spectacularly; to Nancy, my wife of nineteen years, who knows me better than anyone in the world and is the best *kalyanamitra* I could have; to numerous friends who would be surprised or embarrassed to find themselves so listed.

Admittedly, the resources I have catalogued here for constructing a post-modern spiritual discipline sound unpromising —the shards and clinkers of a disintegrating culture, the remnants of previously taken paths, the often preoccupied and theologically unsophisticated people around me. But it is all I have. And it is all anyone has today. If we look for something else, or somewhere else, we will look, I fear, in vain. But I hope that does not discourage us. As a first-century *kalyanamitra* once wrote to a confused little urban *sangha* that was trying to understand a dharma that had recently come from the East, " . . . the divine weakness is stronger than man's strength. To shame the wise, God has chosen what the world counts weakness. He has chosen things low and contemptible, mere nothings, to overthrow the existing order." (I Corinthians 1:26–28)

Bibliography

Anderson, Niels-Erik A., *The Old Testament Sabbath: A Traditional-Historical Investigation*. Dissertation Series #7, for Form Criticism Seminar (Missoula, Montana. Society of Biblical Literature, 1972)

Baba, Pagal, *Temple of the Phallic King, The Mind of India: Yogis, Swamis, Saints and Avatars* (New York: Simon and Schuster, 1973)

Benson, Herbert, *The Relaxation Response* (New York: William Morrow and Co., Inc., 1975)

Berrigan, Daniel and Thich Nhat Hanh, *The Raft Is Not the Shore: Conversations Toward A Buddhist/Christian Awareness* (Boston: Beacon Press, 1975)

Biersdorf, John E., *Hunger for Experience* (New York: Seabury Press, 1975)

Blofeld, John, *The Tantric Mysticism of Tibet* (New York: E. P. Dutton and Co., Inc., 1970)

Bonhoeffer, Dietrich, *Letters and Papers from Prison* (New York: Macmillan, 1967)

Cohen, Daniel, *The New Believers, Young Religion in America* (New York: Evans and Co., 1975)

Corwin, Charles, *East to Eden, Religion and the Dynamics of Social Change* (Grand Rapids: William Eerdmans Publishing Co., 1972)

Danto, Arthur C., *Mysticism and Morality, Oriental Thought and Moral Philosophy* (New York: Basic Books, 1972)

Davy, Marie-Magdeleine, *The Mysticism of Simone Weil* (London: Rockliff, 1951)

Day, Dorothy, "On Pilgrimage" in *The Catholic Worker*, Vol. XLII, No. 9, December 1976

Dubos, Rene, *A God Within* (New York: Charles Scribner's Sons, 1972)

Dumoulin, Heinrich, *A History of Zen Buddhism*. Translated from the German by Paul Peachey (New York: Pantheon Books, 1963)

Eliade, Mircea, *Cosmos and History, The Myth of the Eternal Return*. Translated from the French by W. R. Trask (New York: Harper and Row, 1954)

Ellwood, Robert S., Jr., *Religious and Spiritual Groups in Modern America* (New Jersey: Prentice-Hall, Inc., 1973)

Erikson, Erik, *Identity and the Life Cycle:* Selected Papers, *Psychological Issues*, Monograph #1, Vol. 1, No. 1 (New York: International University Press, 1967)

Guenther, Herbert and Chogyam Trungpa, *The Dawn of Tantra* (Berkeley: Shambala; New York: Random House, distributor, 1975)

Hendin, Herbert, *The Age of Sensation* (New York: Norton, 1975)

Heschel, Abraham Joshua, *The Sabbath*, from *The Earth Is the Lord's* and *The Sabbath* (New York: Harper Torchbook, 1966)

Hillman, James, *Re-Visioning Psychology* (New York: Harper and Row, 1975)

Homans, Peter, "Psychology and Hermeneutics: An exploration of Basic Issues and Resources," from *Journal of Religion*, Vol. 55, No. 3, July 1975, pp. 327–347.

Humphreys, Christmas, *Zen Buddhism* (New York: Macmillan, 1949)

Hyers, M. Conrad, *Zen and the Comic Spirit* (London: Rider and Co., 1973)

Johnston, William, *Christian Zen* (New York: Harper and Row, 1971)

———, *Silent Music: The Science of Meditation* (New York: Harper and Row, 1974)

Judah, J. Stillson, *Hare Krishna and the Counterculture* (New York: John Wiley and Sons, 1974)

Kelley, Dean M., *Why Conservative Churches Are Growing* (New York: Harper and Row, 1972)

Knowles, David, *Christian Monasticism* (London: World University Library, 1969)

MacCormick, Chalmers, "The Zen Catholicism of Thomas Merton," in *Journal of Ecumenical Studies*, Fall 1972, Vol. 9, No. 4.

Maharishi International University, *Science of Creative Intelligence for Secondary Education* (Goleta, California: MIU Press Publication No. G1-184-875, 1975)

Masters, R. E. L., and Jean Houston, *The Varieties of Psychedelic Experience* (New York: Dell Publishing Co., Inc., 1966)

Merton, Thomas, *Mystics and Zen Masters* (New York: Dell Publishing Co., 1961)

———, *Raids on the Unspeakable* (New York: New Directions, 1964)

Myerhoff, Barbara, "The Huichole and the Quest for Paradise," in *Parabola*, Winter, 1976, Vol. 1, Issue 1, pp. 22–29.

———, *Peyote Hunt: The Sacred Journey of the Huichole Indians* (Ithaca: Cornell University Press, 1974)

Naranjo, Claudio, *The One Quest* (New York: Viking Press, 1972)

Naranjo, Claudio and Robert Arnstein, *On the Psychology of Meditation* (New York: Viking Press, 1971)

Needleman, Jacob, *The New Religions* (New York: Doubleday, 1970)

———, *A Sense of the Cosmos: The Encounter of Modern Science and Ancient Truth* (New York: Doubleday, 1975)

Northrop, F. S. C., *The Meeting of East and West: An Inquiry Concerning World Understanding* (New York: Macmillan, 1960)

Parry, J. H., *The European Reconnaissance* (New York: Walker and Co., 1968)

Pope, Harrison, Jr., *The Road East: America's New Discovery of Eastern Wisdom* (Boston: Beacon Press, 1974)

Raskin, Jonah, *The Mythology of Imperialism* (New York: Random House, 1971)

Rupp, George, *Christologies and Cultures: Toward a Typology of Religious Worldviews* (The Hague: Mouton and Co., 1974)

Schleiffer, Hedwig, *Sacred Narcotic Plants of the New World Indians: An Anthology of Texts from the Sixteenth Century to Date* (New York: Macmillan and Co., 1973)

Schneider, Michael, *Neurose und Klassenkampf* (Towohlt, Germany, 1973)

Segundo, Juan Luis, *Our Idea of God*, Vol. 3; Translated by John Drury (Maryknoll, New York: Orbis Books, 1974)

Singer, Isaac Bashevis, *Short Friday and Other Stories* (New York: Farrar, Straus and Giroux, 1961; Signet Books, 1965)

Singer, Milton, *When a Great Tradition Modernizes* (London: Pall Mall Press, 1972)

Snyder, Gary, *Earth House Hold* (New York: New Directions Book, 1957; 1969)

Soelle, Dorothee, *Political Theology*, translated by John Shelley (Philadelphia, Fortress Press, 1974)

Starr, Susan Leigh, "The Politics of Wholeness: A Feminist Critique of the New Spirituality," in *Sinister Wisdom*, Vol. 1, No. 2

Suzuki, Shunryu, *Zen Mind, Beginner's Mind* (New York and Tokyo: Weatherhill, 1973)

Trungpa, Chogyam, *Born in Tibet* (Hammondsworth, Middlesex, England: Penguin Books, 1971)

———, *Cutting Through Spiritual Materialism* (Berkeley: Shambala, 1973)

———, *The Myth of Freedom and the Way of Meditation* (Berkeley and London: Shambala, 1976)

———, in an interview, "Things Get Very Clear When You're Cornered," in *The Laughing Man*, No. 2, 1976, p. 56 (San Francisco: *The Laughing Man*, 1976)

Underhill, Evelyn, *The Mystics of the Church* (New York: Schocken, 1964)

Veblen, Thorstein, *The Theory of the Leisure Class*. Introduction by C. Wright Mills (New York: Mentor Books, New American Library, 1953)

de Ventos, Xavier Rubert, *Self-Defeated Man: Personal Identity and Beyond* (New York: Harper and Row, 1975). Originally published in Spain as *Moral y Nueva Cultura* (Alianza Editorial, 1971)

Weeden, Theodore J., *Mark—Traditions in Conflict* (Philadelphia: Fortress Press, 1971)

Weil, Simone, *Waiting for God* (New York: Harper and Row, 1973)

Wheelis, Allen, *The Quest for Modernity* (New York: W. W. Norton, 1958)

Whitworth, John McK., *God's Blueprints: A Sociological Study of Three Utopian Sects*

Wild, John, *Human Freedom and Social Order* (Durham: University of North Carolina Press, 1959)

Wilder, Amos, *The New Voice* (New York: Harper and Herder, 1969)

Zaehner, R. C., *Our Savage God—The Perverse Use of Eastern Thought* (Mission, Kansas: Sheed and Ward, 1975)

Index